LUNCH
WITH THE
AMERICAN PEOPLE
SATIRICAL FOOD FOR THOUGHT

BY MARTIN H. LEVINSON

NeoPoiesisPress.com

NeoPoiesis Press, LLC

2775 Harbor Ave SW, Suite D, Seattle, WA 98126-2138
Inquiries: Info@NeoPoiesisPress.com
NeoPoiesisPress.com

Martin H. Levinson – Lunch with the American People: Satirical Food for Thought
ISBN 979-8-9858336-2-1 (paperback: alk. paper))

    1. Satire. I. Levinson, Martin. II. Lunch with the American People.

Library of Congress Control Number: 2023933352

First Edition

Cover illustration: Ken Hofbauer

Cover design: Milo Duffin and Stephen Roxborough

Printed in the United States of America.

The people long eagerly for just two
things: bread and circuses!
—Juvenal

Acknowledgments

Thank you: to Dale Winslow and NeoPoiesis Press for providing a platform for these satires and shaping them skillfully into a book; to Dan Geddes, the founder and editor of *The Satirist*, for giving these essays a home over the years; to Lance Strate for his encouragement and support in bringing this book to fruition; to the members of the Westhampton Free Library Writers Group for their comments and critiques on my pieces and a special thanks to Donna Lee McGullam, the leader of the group, for her excellent ideas and suggestions; and to my wife, Katherine Liepe-Levinson for being my fellow idea person, photographer extraordinaire, best friend, and general all around helpmate.

CONTENTS

Foreword

Martin Levinson is a prolific humor writer, and his *Lunch with the American People* collects fifty of his short satirical essays, satires, fictions, and poems from recent years, many of which were first published in *The Satirist*.

Levinson writes satire in a myriad of genres: satires, stories, poems, and essays using different styles, guises, and points of view. The recurring targets of his pieces include: the abysmal state of American political and social discourse; the superficiality of social media; the idiocy of (let's face it) mainly right-wing conspiracy theories; extreme wokeness as a departure from common sense; the decline of education; and many other topical themes.

The satire in this book is informed by acute semantic insight. The title essay, "Lunch with the America People" highlights the weird use of abstractions in political discourse. The narrator is (literally) having lunch with "the American people" in a diner, as if having lunch with such an abstraction (and political cliché) were possible; yet politicians often speak in such abstractions. "At the End of the Day There's Another . . . Cliché" manages to use a cliché in nearly every sentence to point out our overreliance on clichés in everyday language, often as a substitution for thinking. In the poem "The Road I Should Not Have Taken," Levinson captures the cadence of the Frost original in the lament of a driver who failed to listen to the Waze app and got lost. The poem "What the F*ck" is a showcase of the versatility of the f-word in contemporary usage.

Many of the pieces in this volume evince the shallowness of contemporary life, especially of social media in, for example, "In Defense of Facebook," where we hear the argument "Other than people in witness protection programs and drug dealers, who has anything to hide?" In "Three Words Max" (a comment on Twitter's word limitation), we see a series of short, dramatic scenes, where each line in the exchange is only three words. "Influencers from the Bible" employs anachronism by presenting Old Testament characters as social media influencers, showing us that when discussing human nature there is nothing new under the sun. "Reviewing Paperclips" captures the absurdity of online shopping and customer service experiences. "The Wisdom of the Crowd" offers an historical survey on the perils of groupthink.

Levinson relishes ridiculing conspiracy theories. In "Trump Wuz Robbed," which lampoons some absurd electoral fraud claims, we read the fake news that: "In Pennsylvania, the night before the election, a bunch of Quakers, Amish people, Philadelphia Phillies fans, EMILY's list supporters, Bryn Mawr students, and members of Antifa drove the length and breadth of the Keystone State warning Republican voters to not show up at the polls the following day." In "LMNOPAnon" we read the secret intel "LMNOPAnon discovered that on October 7, 2019, German Prime Minister Angela Merkel, French President Emmanuel Macron, and Chinese Premier Xi Jinping met and developed a plan that involved eating the children of Trump supporters." In "Breaking and Entering Tourism," we find an uproarious take on the twisted apologists for the January 6 Capitol break-in: "a new type of international travel for adventurous sightseers where you not only get to see famous buildings, you get to uniquely interact with what's inside them" in such travel adventures as "Breaking into Parliament," "Busting into the Louvre," and "Bouncing into the UN."

Levinson often takes the satirical tack of inhabiting the views of those he wishes to satirize. In "Say it Loud, I'm Anti Vax and I'm Proud," we see an "anti-vaxxer" chronicling an alternate history of vaccination and getting it all very wrong. ("The Democrats said the problem wasn't largepox. It was smallpox, a disease they made up.") In "It's Five O'Clock Somewhere" it's proposed that the banalities of social interaction during happy hour get rebranded as "Tribal Loyalty Hour," "Schadenfreude Hour" and "Bitching Hour," as happy hours often degenerate into these rather than happy times anyway.

As a satirist, Levinson "punches up" in pieces such as "Hail the 'One Percent,' " which finds historical, Biblical, and economic justifications for the absurd concentration of wealth in recent years. In "Fifty Shades of Green," we see a rich couple on a date saturated with more elite brand-consciousness than in *American Psycho*. Former President Trump is also a frequent satirical target in pieces such as "The Donald J. Trump Presidential Library," in which we tour through the horrors of "The Pantheon of Outstanding Political Appointees," "The Hall of Tweets," and "The Deal Killing Room."

Levinson addresses the delicate contemporary issue of wokeness in such satires as "Dinner at the Woke Street Café" and "Safe Space University." At Safe Space University, we find that "The Office is staffed with lawyers, psychologists, harmful-speech investigators, and specially trained dogs that can determine whether a person who is dog whistling is sending out subtly aimed political messages or is simply using a high-pitched whistle to train a dog." Levinson bemoans the decline of educational standards in "Farewell the Three "R's" and "Privatizing Schools for Fun and Profit."

Satirists are often loosely divided into the Juvenalian (bitter, pessimistic) vs. Horatian (warmer, more tolerant of humanity's foibles). Levinson writes predominantly in a tolerant, Horatian tone, which is a welcome relief from the often-poisoned social and political discourse of our time. His latest volume of satire gently asks us to look again at the inconceivable folly of our society and politics. The ability to laugh at ourselves is one of the best techniques we possess to heal the wounds that divide "the American people."

Dan Geddes
Editor, *The Satirist*
May 7, 2022

Introduction

Through the ages, satire has involved holding up vice and folly to ridicule and scorn. Its literary use dates back to the ancient Greeks but the Romans are considered the first true satirists. When it came to immorality, crime, and the misuse of wealth, Roman satirists dished out derision like nobody's business.

Jonathan Swift wrote blistering satire. His most famous satirical essay, *A Modest Proposal* (1729), argues that parents with little means should sell their children as food. The piece mocked heartless, upper-class British attitudes toward the poor as well as British policy toward the Irish.

In the 19th century, Mark Twain used humorous exaggeration and irony to expose people's failings and narcissism—a favorite Twain line: "Be respectful of your superiors, if you have any." In the last century, Sinclair Lewis, H.L. Mencken, and Tom Wolfe used satire to comment on rigid American middle-class mores, and Aldous Huxley and George Orwell used it to make cutting observations on authoritarian rule.

Nowadays, television comedians Bill Maher and Steven Colbert employ satire in monologues and discussions on their shows. The ensemble cast of *Saturday Night Live* and the cartoon show *South Park* also use satire through skits and stories that make tongue-in-cheek observations on individuals and society.

The internet abounds with satire. Noteworthy examples can be found by clicking on *The Onion* (a cyberspace journal that bills itself as "America's Finest News Source"), *The Satirist,* and *The Borowitz Report.*

This book continues satire's long tradition of exposing iniquity and foolishness to scorn and mockery. The short pieces in it make fun of a wide array of targets ranging from politics and social affairs to holiday newsletters to self-improvement hucksterism. Each was written to encourage the reader to think more deeply about the topic being discussed and to laugh or cry a little over the idiosyncrasies inherent in the human comedy, which never disappoint in supplying fodder for satire.

Please note that perusing these satires may cause your mind to expand and your nervous system to register feelings of delight. Do not be alarmed if you experience these effects. They are rarely long lasting and real life is the perfect antidote.

Photograph by Katherine Liepe-Levinson

PART 1: POLITICS

Lunch with the American People

Yesterday I had lunch with the American people. I had wanted to speak with them for the longest time, as they are a highly influential group of folks often mentioned by politicians on TV news programs.

I met the people at a diner near where I live. I ordered a BLT sandwich with coleslaw on the side and a cup of coffee. The people ordered cheeseburger specials with double fries and Diet Cokes. I told the waitress to give everyone separate checks.

After some idle chitchat about the huge portions of food typically served in diners, I asked the American people to tell me their thoughts on wearing masks and getting vaccinated to prevent Covid. They started to answer the question before I could finish it and the cacophony and contempt that individuals within the group had for those who did not share their views was certifiably crazy. Luckily, I had a whistle in my pocket and after blowing it as loud as I could the crowd calmed down. It turned out 30% of the people thought mask wearing and taking shots to prevent Covid was a bad idea, 50% thought it was a good idea, 10% said it was a good idea on weekdays but a bad one on weekends, 7% had no opinion on the matter, and 3% said the pandemic was fake news. I moved on to illegal immigration.

"Do you think a security fence should be built on the Mexican border? Do you support a guest worker program? Are you in favor of granting amnesty to undocumented individuals currently living in the United States?"

The people popped right in with answers, which they argued about forcefully with each other, some waving knives and forks in their hands. I worried it might get physical so, after again blowing hard on my whistle, I told everyone to calm down and give a little thought to what they were saying. But I was advised that's not how American's roll. One guy said, "We are not a nation of deliberators. We know what we think and want to express our views quickly so we don't get confused in case someone interrupts us with different ideas."

I pleaded with the people to keep their voices low, warning if they didn't we might be asked to leave. That entreaty worked, and was helped by having our food brought out from the kitchen. As the plates were being set down, the people began to argue about who should sit where. I said I didn't think it mattered where anyone sat and while they were debating the issue their food was getting cold. No one seemed to care about that and the squabbling continued so I took out my trusty whistle, gave it a blow, and said, "How about we stop the bickering and just enjoy the meal," to which I was told "Mind your own business and pass the salt."

I had wanted to talk to the people about the economy, race relations, abortion, and a host of other topics but I didn't have the strength to keep blowing my whistle. That a third of the American people were packing guns also made me wary to talk about anything that was controversial. So I decided to talk about something that was innocuous. "Nice weather we're having," I said to my tablemates.

Meteorology was not the conversational safe harbor I thought it would be. Some of the people said the weather did not look nice to them, others accused me of being a climate-change denier, and a few demanded to know why I was talking about the weather when there were so many more interesting and important subjects we could talk about. Rather than respond to their remarks I requested the checks.

The checks totaled two billion dollars, minus the tips; not a bad price for three hundred thirty million cheese-burger specials. The bad part was the only thing everyone agreed on was that I should pay for the food. I didn't want to fight such a petulant throng so I agreed to pick up the tab, which didn't make me happy, as the limit on my credit card is ten thousand dollars.

I asked the waitress if I could pay with a personal check. She said I could as long as I had three forms of photo ID. Fortunately, I did.

As I got into my car to go home two thoughts struck me. The next time I speak to the American people I will do it on Twitter, where you don't have to feed folks to get them to talk and you can be as outlandish, unthinking, and arbitrary as you like; and after my check bounces, I doubt if I will ever be welcomed to eat at this diner again.

In Defense of Facebook

Facebook believes people are kind and sweet. That's why it has no problem with individuals organizing insurrections, distributing false information to sway elections, and canceling folks who have made a mistake in their lives. It's all about compassion and concern. From its very beginnings in 2003, when Mark Zuckerberg created an online program at Harvard that allowed users to objectify fellow students by comparing photos of their faces and selecting who they deemed as "hotter," Facebook has sought to increase love and understanding in the world.

One way it does this is by encouraging everyone to know everything about everybody, which is a wonderful thing because if people keep information about themselves private, how can you get to know who they really are. Other than people in witness protection programs and drug dealers, who has anything to hide? Your life should be an open book and people should be able to look into that book and if they find a typo they should warn others about it. Everyone and their mother, who is probably also on Facebook, should have a chance to review your manuscript.

Cynics say Facebook's goal isn't to provide users a place to connect with friends and family but rather a place to sell ad space to companies. "Facecrook," they say, is a virtual stalker who wants to see what you like so they can monetize it.

Hey, if Facebook can make a little dough from the data they collect from you and then sell it to others what's the big deal. People should be flattered that a mega corporation is willing to take the time and effort to track both users and nonusers on other sites and apps. Who else in your life, other than perhaps a partner you are in the process of separating from or the Internal Revenue Service, is interested in following you around on the internet.

Facebook's algorithms are finely tuned to favor content that creates strong emotional reactions that bar any hope of rational analysis. And that's great because reason had its day with the Enlightenment. Today it's all about fear and outrage, emotions Facebook's news feed is more than happy to oblige with dramatic, attention-grabbing leads that bypass the cortex and go directly to the amygdala, a word that if you don't know you can look up on your smartphone.

Speaking of smart, Facebook has figured out how to increase their users' enjoyment by bringing together groups of likeminded people who don't mind if their members post weird, crazy, and even demonstrably false messages. Tribal loyalty trumps verisimilitude, which is as it should be because faithfulness is a virtue and what is truth but a five-letter word fit for crossword puzzles and Scrabble.

Every Facebook user has a chance to voice their opinions and have those opinions spread like wildfire across the virtual world. Dousing those conflagrations so they don't lead people to go crazy over the incessant stream of stressful news in their Facebook feed and punt on taking vaccines that could save their lives is not Facebook's, or anyone else's, problem. These are small prices to pay for a social media service that keeps people away from the horrors of thinking deeply about themselves and what is going on in the world. Doing those things can only come to no good and will cause a person to be trolled on Twitter, teased on TikTok, made fun of on Instagram, and result in the total demise of contemporary civilization as we know it.

Say It Loud, I'm Anti Vax and I'm Proud

When the smallpox vaccine was invented in the 18th century, it didn't prevent people from getting sick with smallpox, it just wasted everyone's time because people weren't getting sick with smallpox. They were getting sick from "largepox," a malady caused by big, visible, airborne particles that can easily be warded off by ducking or turning your back when you see them coming. That's what George Washington, the first president of the American Republic and by virtue of that fact a Republican, told people to do. But there were others with different ideas.

The Democrats said the problem wasn't largepox, it *was* smallpox, a disease they made up. They said you couldn't see smallpox and the best way to avoid it was to get vaccinated. The Dems convinced the head of the CCDC (Centers for Colonial Disease Control) to send horseback riders to towns and villages to tell people to get the jab, which resulted in lots of sore arms and tons of time lost from drinking beer, rum, and hard cider at the local taverns. You couldn't trust the Democrats then, and you can't trust them now.

The measles vaccine, which was developed in the 1960s, was also a scam. The Sixties was a time of great protest in society, and it wasn't only people who protested. The germs that cause measles also protested by not infecting people and carrying placards at rallies that read "Microbes Against Measles" and "Hey, Hey, ho, ho, getting sick has got to go." The result was very few people got measles in the Sixties. And that was not just because of a bunch of picketing microorganisms.

In 1953, Dr. Jonas Salk announced on a national radio news show that he had successfully tested a vaccine against poliomyelitis, the virus that causes the crippling disease of polio. What he didn't announce was that people were already being protected against polio by eating Twinkies. It turned out that in 1953 a secret additive was being put into Twinkies that prevented polio. How that additive got into the cake mix and who placed it there remains a mystery to this day but research done by the International Disease and Dessert Association (IDDA) has shown that the extract killed the virus.

Now the government wants people to get shots to prevent Covid. But it's not what's in the shot that's keeping people from contracting Covid; it's the placebo effect that's preventing them from getting the disease. Folks receiving the vaccine believe it will work and in response their bodies create antibodies to fight the virus. It's called the mind-body connection. Look it up.

In this time of pestilence we need to have trust that we are stronger than an itsy-bitsy, teensy-weensy, two-bit bug. We will get through this pandemic with perseverance, pluck, not being pussies, and eventually herd immunity. The virus will not beat us. In the sage words of a former US president: "It's going to disappear. One day—it's like a miracle—it will disappear."

Trump Wuz Robbed

A majority of Republicans believe there was widespread fraud in the 2020 presidential election. They're right of course but, like the rest of the country, they don't know the half of it. Well, let me fill everyone in.

In Pennsylvania, the night before the election, a bunch of Quakers, Amish people, Philadelphia Phillies fans, EMILY's list supporters, Bryn Mawr students, and members of Antifa drove the length and breadth of the Keystone State warning Republican voters to not show up at the polls the following day. They said if they did appear, their children would be taken from them and sent to work at a child-sex ring operated by Hillary Clinton in the basement of a pizzeria in Washington, DC. They also said if they were caught voting they would be smeared on the internet as Democrats and doubters of the homilies of Hannity, the teachings of Tucker, the imaginings of Ingraham, and the orations of O'Reilly.

In Georgia, pecan pies were mailed to registered Republican voters a month before the election with microchips embedded in them that when ingested would cause a person to pull the lever for Joe Biden on Election Day. The pies were accompanied by a note saying they were a gift from Donald Trump, who wanted Georgians to know he was sweet on their state and wished to share his good feelings with people who desired to make America great again, like it was before 1865.

In Wisconsin, Democratic Party hacks based in Madison and Milwaukee scrubbed Trump's name off ballots that were then sent to rural precincts in the Badger State.

On Election Day, when voters complained about the deletions, they were told if they wanted to vote for Trump they could write his name in on the ballot. What they were not told was they were writing his name with invisible ink—unbeknownst to Wisconsin voters, Barbra Streisand, Jane Fonda, Tom Hanks, and members of the Black Lives Matter movement had bribed election officials throughout America's Dairyland to have invisible-ink pens used at their polling places. Needless to say, Trump write-in votes weren't counted.

In Michigan, Michael Moore, Alexandria Ocasio-Cortez, Rashida Tlaib, Karl Marx, Groucho Marx, Chico Marx, Harpo Marx, Zeppo Marx, Gummo Marx, and thousands of other Marxists snuck into polling sites on election eve and rigged the voting machines to register Trump votes as Biden votes. That same night, a group of LGBT nihilists drove around the Great Lake State and punctured tires of cars owned by Republicans, which meant many of those car owners were flat out of luck getting to the polls the next day.

In Arizona, drug dealers, Mexican rapists, people who kneel during the national anthem at sporting events, women who resist being grabbed by the pussy, Anderson Cooper, and a bunch of Latin American immigrants formed caravans that traveled to polling sites in the Grand Canyon State where they voted early and often. When they were questioned why their names were not on the voting rolls, they produced forged letters from Sheriff Joe Arpaio saying the reason was because of a bureaucratic error. The letters also said that their bearers were true-blue Arizonans who believed in racially profiling Latinos, denying prisoners

13

basic human rights in jails, and in the rudimentary notion that you can't have too many guns, votes, or presidential pardons.

All these instances of election fraud were presented at the sixty-plus court challenges that Trump mounted after the election but they did not sway the judges because the magistrates had been put under a spell by Democratic operatives disguised as bailiffs who hypnotized them into dismissing the evidence.

But Trump is planning a comeback and talking freely about being reinstated. He already has a slogan to run on: "It's morning in America: time to toast some white bread, deport some Mexicans, grab an AR-15, and make America even greater than it was when I was illegally forced out of office in 2020." No way he can lose with a slogan like that.

LMNOPAnon

Everyone knows about *QAnon*, a rightwing, internet conspiracy theory whose mission is to unearth the secret plots that the deep state has hatched against Donald Trump and his supporters. What is less well-known, and of far greater relevance to American politics, is *LMNOPAnon*, a sister conspiracy theory that has uncovered evidence showing that Democrats are secret Satan-worshippers and the Democratic Party, abetted by Beelzebub, is trying to get rid of organized religion and make America a secular state.

LMNOPAnon has found the deep state is not America's biggest problem. The biggest threat to the country is that in our two-party political system one of the parties is in league with the devil, immigrants, black people, brown people, yellow people, people sporting other colors, and people who think voting should be made easy.

Democracy as a way of life was baked in the cake when the Constitution was written in 1787, with white men having the exclusive right to vote. But during the Civil War, the great-great grandparents of George Soros and a claque of nineteenth-century globalists met with Abraham Lincoln to rig the Constitution so black men could vote. A little more than fifty years later, a crowd of Hollywood liberals and pro-choice supporters cut a deal with Woodrow Wilson that gave women the franchise. Four years after that, a bunch of Antifa supporters and politically correct college professors bribed Congress to let the Indians get in on the ballot. Today, the US electorate is a rainbow of rapscallions with white men a minority of voters.

Worse things have happened than the weakening of white male control at the ballot box. For example, LMNOPAnon discovered that in 2019, German Prime Minister Angela Merkel, French President Emmanuel Macron, and Chinese Premier Xi Jinping met and developed a plan that involved eating the children of Trump supporters. Here's how the scheme worked.

Text messages were sent to children of Trump allies, inviting the youngsters to a pizza and ice cream party at the United Nations' Delegates Dining Room in New York City. When the kids showed up to the gathering they were fed pizza and ice cream laced with arsenic, which caused them to have horrible stomachaches and die. Their bodies were then taken to JFK airport and flown to Berlin, Paris, and Beijing where they were baked into meat pies and served at state banquets in those capitals. The idea was to provide diners at these events with a one-of-a-kind culinary experience and to get revenge on people who voted into office a man who attacked the French, Germans, and Chinese bigly.

Trump was supportive of LMNOPAnon in its desire to destroy democracy and stop the Democrats from gaining power. He was also onto the UN cannibalism caper. In his last year in office, he sent a bill to Congress that required invitations to children's pizza and ice cream parties be accompanied by sworn affidavits saying that unadulterated pizza and ice cream would be served at those celebrations. Due to Democrat obstruction, the bill is still in committee.

Hail the "One Percent"

People like to complain about the *one percent*, those individuals whose net worth is a lot more than yours. But the ultra rich are not that different from those who inveigh against them. To paraphrase Shakespeare: If you prick them, do they not bleed? If you poison them, do they not die? If you ask them to contribute their fair share of taxes to keep the country running, do they not comply? Okay, maybe not the last one, but two out of three ain't bad.

What would happen if the "one percent" decided to not spend their money and squirrel it away instead? Say goodbye to $200-million-dollar luxury yachts and Patek Philippe Grandmaster Chime watches. Say goodbye to Bugatti Centodiecis and Mercedes AMG-One cars. Say goodbye to Briolette diamond necklaces and Peacock brooches by Graff.

And what if the one-percenters got tired of being dissed and dismissed and decamped to Monte Carlo, Capri, or some other glitzy place outside America? Say goodbye to jobs in this country for private chauffeurs, private butlers, private maids, and private parts (just kidding here). Say goodbye to Sotheby's, Christie's, and Phillips Auction House. Say hello to no one to rag on for having loads of lucre and spending it in ludicrous ways.

Some people aspire to things other than making tons of dough. Things like teaching children, caring for the sick, and working with the poor. What do you think would happen if everyone had those aspirations? Nothing would happen since the scenario just described could never happen because contrary to what you learned in school, it's money makes the world go round.

Even the Bible subscribes to that philosophy. The proverb "Man shall not live by bread alone" is God's way of saying you need more than just the basics to survive. Life requires high-end luxury goods, a point that is expanded on in the Book of Bezos 2:34: "And the Lord said, be so rich that you can afford to go to outer space and when you return to Earth still have enough money to buy over 140 foreign countries."

Donald Trump, a celebrated cleric in the church of the almighty dollar, says those that have the big bucks have been blessed and those who don't shall not make it into the Kingdom of Heaven, a place he calls Trump Tower North. It's hard to argue that it is better to be a rich grandee than a poor schmuck. If you are in the latter category you should be asking the Almighty for redemption rather than railing against the anointed one-percent. God does not like complainers.

The Donald J. Trump
Presidential Library (2050)

Welcome to the Donald J. Trump Presidential Library located in the lobby of Trump Tower Moscow right next to Comrade Tucker Carlson's Vodka and Blinis Bar. To make your visit more pleasant, the following is a brief description of some of the rooms and attractions inside the building.

The Pantheon of Outstanding Political Appointees contains portraits of Michael Flynn, Scott Pruitt, Tom Price, Jeff Sessions, Anthony Scaramucci, Ryan Zinke, Steve Bannon, Sean Spicer, and other notable Trump Administration officials who were either indicted or forced to leave their jobs. Next to their pictures are brief accounts of the questionable behavior they engaged in while working for the government as well as ballots where you can rate each individual on a head explosion scale that goes from "great" to "frankly unbelievable." Photos may be taken in this room and so may antidepressants and antiemetics if you have them with you.

The Hall of Tweets showcases prominent tweets issued by DJT, many of them when he was in the Oval or on an oval. Such tweets include Trump telling Kim Jong-un that his nuclear button is bigger than Kim's, Trump's 2018 post-election tweet about how he received "so many Congratulations from so many on our Big Victory last night" (a win that resulted in a 40-seat pickup for the Democrats), and the famous "covfefe" tweet that baffled the

19

entire internet and pretty much every one else on the planet.

The Deal-Killing Room features descriptions of deals the president killed (e.g., the Iran Nuclear deal, the Trans-Pacific Partnership, the Paris Climate Change Accord) or modified (e.g., renaming NAFTA as the United States-Mexico-Canada Agreement) to tarnish President Barack Obama's legacy. The room also contains a video collage that shows the president's Herculean efforts over many months to have Congress kill the Affordable Care Act and the refusal of the Supreme Court to be an accessory to the murder.

The Walls "R" Us Annex requires a passport or a valid American visa for entry. The Annex contains photographs of walls from around the world whose purpose is or was to keep others out. These photos include shots of the Great Wall of China, Hadrian's Wall, the Berlin Wall, the Wall on the West Bank in Israel, and the op-ed page of the *Wall Street Journal*. Pink Floyd's 1979 iconic song *The Wall* provides background music for this exhibit, which Mexico was asked to pay for. They declined that request but it didn't matter because the president's base crowdsourced the expense.

The Trump Tower Escalator is a working replica of the escalator Donald Trump descended on before walking up to a podium on June 16, 2015 and announcing his presidential candidacy. Riding down it you will see TV footage from the *Access Hollywood* tape where DJT talks about grabbing women by the pussy, video of campaign rallies with crowds yelling "Lock Her Up," and photos showing shocked and frightened expressions from Hillary

20

Clinton supporters and the bulk of the American people who watched in horror and astonishment as the presidential election results rolled in on the night of November 8, 2016.

The Putin Portico is a ruby-red entryway that features fifty Fabergè eggs detailed with enameled portraits of Donald Trump speaking to his supporters and an eight thousand square-foot mural showing Russian hackers at work on their computers. The portico, designed by Steve Bannon and Paul Manafort, had no collusion in its construction and former Attorney General Bill Barr has said there was also no obstruction. Restrooms are located directly to the right of the portico, next to the statues of Vladimir Lenin, Joseph Stalin, Vladimir Putin, and a host of other ruthless Russians.

The Pandemic Piazza contains videos of Donald Trump addressing maskless political rallies, Donald Trump suggesting that bleach and sunlight might kill the coronavirus, and Donald Trump playing golf while simultaneously coordinating America's response to the Covid pandemic, the upshot of which was a nation that had the greatest number of Covid cases in the world because, as DJT said often during his presidency, we are the greatest nation in the world.

The Mar-a-Lago Special Membership Deal Arcade is staffed by handsome men and beautiful women who, if you present them your admission ticket, will let you in on the deal of a lifetime, namely the ability to receive a substantial discount (a tenth of a percent) off the regular twenty-million-dollar annual Mar-a-Lago membership fee. Your admission ticket will also allow you to enter a special drawing whose prize is an opportunity to play golf with former President Trump. If you win that prize, please be aware that DJT keeps score and guests buy lunch.

The Grift Shop is a great place to spend your rubles on Trump Library souvenirs. One of their more popular items are reproductions of the personal, gold-plated toilet that Donald Trump uses when he spends time in his condominium on the 819th floor of this building. The shop also sells Ivanka Trump's specially formulated beluga caviar skin cream (a unique beauty product that can be applied to the skin or eaten), Republican Senator nesting dolls (each one smaller than the other), and Momma Putin's freeze-dried borscht (an excellent starter to a meal that involves gobbling up and occupying countries next door to yours). As you exit the grift shop, don't forget to give the Monument to the Unknown Pussy a rub for good luck.

Breaking and Entering Tourism

Commenting on the January 2021 Capitol break-in, Georgia representative Andrew Clyde (R) said, "If you didn't know the TV footage was a video from January 6th, you would actually think it was a normal tourist visit." He was widely criticized for that remark but he shouldn't have been. He should have been praised for introducing the world to "Breaking and Entering Tourism," a new type of world travel for adventurous sightseers where you not only get to see famous buildings, you get to uniquely interact with what's inside them. Here's a sampling of how this kind of global vacationing could be promoted.

Breaking into Parliament

The British Parliament is housed in the Palace of Westminster, an iconic London landmark dating back to the 11th century. Tickets are sold during the day to see the place. But if you smash a window at the rear of the residence and climb through it, you can skip buying a ticket and the wait online that often precedes such a purchase.

Once inside the building, head straight to the Parliament floor, grab the speaker's mace, and launch into a diatribe against the European Union and the importance of Brexit. The Tories will love you for it and the Labor Party has hardly any members so any booing from them will be drowned out by the opposition. When you finish your speech, go to an office of one of the lawmakers, sit in their chair, light up a cigar, plant your feet on the desk, and take a selfie. Then filch a laptop or two, bear-spray any Bobbies blocking your way out, and beat it to the street. Next stop, crashing your way into the Tower of London to see the Crown Jewels.

Busting into the Louvre

The Louvre is the world's largest art museum and an historic landmark in Paris, France. It is best known for being the home of the Mona Lisa, a half-length portrait painting by a famous Italian artist who is very well thought of by the culturati. Lots of people want to see this painting, which requires one to get a ticket to enter the museum— but not if you bust into the joint at two in the morning! Do that and, except for a few guards who will probably be asleep, you'll have the place to yourself. Not only will you be able to see the Mona Lisa, you will be able to paint a mustache or beard on her face. Afterward, check out the Greek statue of a naked, armless woman called the Venus de Milo, works by Michelangelo (I'm talking about the artist not the kitchenware manufacturer), and other cool pieces of art that are ripe for defacement.

When you finish looking at the art, make some of your own by drawing graffiti on the gallery walls that explain how great America is and how France should be appreciative for all the aid we gave the French People during the French Revolution. Then dash out the door, find a bistro, and chow down on a buttered brioche, classic French omelette, and a steaming cup of café au lait. There's nothing like a good breakfast to help one celebrate an evening of cultural sacrilege.

Bouncing into the UN

The United Nations headquarters in New York City is home to a horrible den of thieves. But the architecture's not bad and if you are traveling to the Big Apple it is well worth seeing, and messing up. The easiest way to accomplish both those things is to tunnel into the building in the dead of night armed with a machete and a blowtorch.

First stop should be the office of the Secretary-General, which is located in the Secretariat building, a 39-story skyscraper that during the day is filled with secretaries. When you finish overturning the furniture, emptying wastebaskets on the floor, and generally trashing the office, proceed to the room where the General Assembly meets and work your destructive magic there. If you get bored, take a break and post pictures of the damage you're causing so all your friends and followers can see your disdain for diplomats. Alternatively, go to the Security Council Room and issue a resolution condemning the 2020 US presidential election as rigged and ask that sanctions be placed on Joe Biden and his family.

The simplest way to leave is the way you came in and as you exit make sure to defecate on the floor. That's what the B & E tourists did at the US Capitol on January 6, 2020 to register their anger at Congress, and because shit happens. If anyone complains about what you're doing just say there is plenty of crap going on at the UN and you are simply adding to it.

If you will be in New York City for more than a day you might want to consider visiting other tourist attractions like the Empire State Building, Rockefeller Center, and the Statue of Liberty. That last venue is a particularly good one to break into since liberty is what breaking and entering tourism is all about.

Let's Not Make a Monumental Mistake

Why the push to remove Confederate monuments? Those memorials were erected to honor brave American patriots who in the nineteenth century saw that the deep state was a threat to individual liberty and the best way to remedy that was to secede. And secede they did, but not in a nasty, mean-spirited way. They seceded with grace and decorum, giving a 21-gun salute to Fort Sumter as they left the Union, which is why the contretemps that resulted from their withdrawal is called the "Civil" War.

Some argue that the leaders of the Confederacy were traitors who, rather than being honored with monuments, should have been tried for treason. But that sort of thinking only works if you use a standard dictionary definition of "traitor" or the US Constitution's definition of "treason." If you ditch those definitional impediments you could argue that the leaders of the Confederacy were principled partisans trying to keep the homeland safe by attending to business in their home states.

To remove the Confederate monuments would be like erasing history and saying that the Civil War was never fought. While studies done by historians at the College of Alternative Facts have found lots of evidence to support that supposition, liberals don't think that was the case so they should be fighting to keep the Confederate monuments up.

Sadly, statues are not the only Confederate symbols on the chopping block. There have been calls to eliminate the names of Confederates from US military installations, which would be tantamount to admitting it wasn't a good idea to put those names on those installations in the first place. But it was a good idea, as it showed the US military was so confident in its fighting abilities that it was not afraid to name its facilities after the people it had defeated. Rather than removing the names of Confederate leaders from military bases, the military should consider adding the names of other enemy leaders to military posts. There could be a Fort Osama bin Laden, Fort Ho Chi Minh, and Camp Castro.

According to The US Office of Statuary, Trellises, and Garden Plants it costs around $500,000 to do away with your average horseback riding, sword holding, son of the South shall rise again statue. That's a lot of money that could be more usefully spent on other things like rubber bullets, pepper spray, and armored Humvees to stop protests against police violence.

The US Daughters of the Confederacy, an association of Southern women founded in Nashville in 1894 whose stated mission has been the funding and erection of memorials to Confederate soldiers, has labored tirelessly over the years to pay homage to those who fought to keep black people enslaved. Banishing Confederate statutes would be a total repudiation of their work. On May 30, 2020, the organization's headquarters in Richmond was set ablaze during protests over the killing of George Floyd. Why add insult to injury by removing the things that define this group's very existence.

Doing away with Confederate monuments would lead to pain and suffering for bigots, neo-Nazis, and white supremacists all across this wonderful land. But America is better than that. This should be a time of healing and a time to try to make the country great again, or at last not as bad as it would be if the electoral college was abolished and everyone's vote counted equally in presidential elections.

Keep those monuments up! It's the (alt) right thing to do.

The Wisdom of the Crowd

If two heads are better than one, then four heads would be better than two, eight better than four, and so on with regard to getting lots of heads together to come up with smart solutions. Tons of wisdom can emanate from large groups of people and such wisdom has been demonstrated many times over during the course of human history. To wit:

In the spring of 1692, a group of young girls in Salem, Massachusetts claimed to be possessed by the devil and accused several local women of witchcraft. The village burghers, decent God-fearing folks who believed children should be seen, and also heard, convened a special court in Salem to hear the cases.

The first convicted witch, Bridget Bishop, was hanged in June. Eighteen others followed Bishop to Salem's Gallows Hill, while some 150 men, women, and children were accused of witchcraft over the next several months. Years later, the citizens of Salem had second thoughts about how they handled the issue and in 1711 they passed a bill exonerating those executed as witches, showing that crowds can course correct if need be.

The French Revolution (1789-1794) demonstrated "the people" are wise in ways still being talked about today. It is a textbook example of how a potpourri of partisans, working steadily and with firm determination, can spice up everyday existence and provide world-class entertainment to those it purports to represent.

To oust the aristocracy, and get rid of anyone accused of being an aristocrat, the peasants got together and using an innovative, state-of-the-art head-removing device, beheaded tens of thousands of Frenchmen, Frenchwomen, and French children. For good measure, the architect of the revolution's reign of terror, the radical Jacobin Maximilien Robespierre, also received a razor cut. But guillotining proved an insufficient means for the downtrodden to attain their ends so public beatings, firing squads, and weighting victims and tossing them from boats were added to the mix. A good time was had by all and the cherry on the cake was the rise of Napoleon, who turned out to be a more ruthless despot than Louis XVI, the king the people had deposed.

In 1921, packs of white residents burned the Greenwood district of Tulsa (popularly known as "America's Black Wall Street") to the ground in one of the single worst occurrences of racial violence in America's history.

The incident that touched off the riot was an accusation that a young African-American shoe shiner had assaulted a white female elevator operator. The alleged offender was arrested and taken to jail. But everyone understood black people like being incarcerated because they are treated like royalty in prison. If justice were to be done, the white residents of Tulsa would have to be the ones to do it.

Throngs of white folks made their way to where the perpetrator was being held and carefully argued the pros and cons of what they thought should be happen in the matter. The conclusion they arrived at was perfectly brilliant: destroy one of the most successful black communities in America. And destroy they did, leaving scores of black people dead, more than 1,400 homes and businesses burned, and nearly 10,000 people homeless.

Shortly after the carnage there was a brief official inquiry, but documents related to the affair vanished soon thereafter. The Tulsa race massacre never received widespread attention and for many decades was not included in the history books used to teach Oklahoma's schoolchildren—more evidence of the wisdom of the crowd, in this case a crowd of racist politicians, bureaucrats, and educators.

Early in the day, on January 6, 2021, an assemblage of American patriots gathered on the Ellipse in Washington DC where they were told by soon-to-be ex-president Donald Trump, "You can never take our country back with weakness." Struck by the sagacity of that remark, and its clear implication that pusillanimity among the people would result in Congress ratifying Joe Biden as president of the United Station, the multitude marched to the Capitol and outside its hallowed halls engaged in Socratic dialogue about best steps to take going forward. The steps they chose were the ones leading up to the entrance of the Capitol, which they climbed with deep conviction in the righteousness of their cause, smashing their way through windows and doors as they entered into the nation's temple of democracy.

Once inside, these icons of valor and courage lined up in an orderly manner and, with great veneration for our nation's legislature, proceeded to wreck the place. For good measure, after paying respect to the Speaker of the House by ransacking her files and grabbing laptops from her office, some of the group defecated on the Capitol

31

floor as they exited the edifice. Such extraordinary wisdom, followed by such impressive action, has rarely been seen from such a sizable group of flag-waving merrymakers and if substantial numbers of this cohort are convicted for the breaking and entering crimes they have been accused of, it may be a long time before we see such collective genius on the national stage again.

Word Up!

From the Boston Tea Party to the insurrection at the US Capitol in 2021, Americans have always been partisan and headstrong. Some have explained this by saying that it is in our genes and cultural DNA to act that way and TV and social media have made the problem worse. But I believe the explanation for why Americans are opinionated and temperamental is simpler than that: it's English, with its histrionic parts of speech that lead us to be rancorous and divisive. Case in point, proper nouns.

Proper nouns, because they are spelled with initial capital letters, think they are better than all the other nouns, which they label as common. The "common" nouns understandably hate that tag and try to get back at the proper nouns wherever and whenever they can. When proper nouns are used in a sentence the common ones will often mock them as being condescending, snobbish, stick-in-the-muds. Sometimes they will put a banana peel in the middle of a sentence just to see if they can get a proper noun to slip on it and cause the sentence to fragment.

Possessive nouns are nouns that claim proprietorship over other words, using apostrophes to get the job done (e.g., the cat's toy, John's book, Betty's land). When different grammatical constructions are used instead of them (e.g., the toy the cat has, the book John owns, the land Betty possesses) they will often become distressed and throw hissy fits. Possessive nouns are no fun to be with at parties because when anyone speaks about anything they assert ownership over the topic being discussed.

Reflexive pronouns (himself, herself, myself, etc.) are not *pro* nouns. Rather, they are pro themselves and reflexively don't care about any other parts of speech. Reflexive pronouns think they are the hottest things going. Instead of quietly and thoughtfully functioning by their lonesome as noun phrases, these jokers get their jollies by letting every word within linguistic hailing distance know it's all about them. When having discussions, they typically talk only about themselves—or any of the other words ending in "self" or "selves."

Let's look at verbs. When an action verb is transitive it is followed by a direct object, for example, "let's eat pie." When an action verb is intransitive, it does not have a direct object, to wit, "let's eat." Each of these verb classes thinks their way of handling objects is the correct one. Because of that conviction, when transitive verbs and intransitive verbs get thrown together in the same paragraph there is often hell to pay and interjections such as "Yipes!" or "What!" get bandied about.

Speaking of interjections, these utterances invariably piss off all the other syntactical categories, as they are viewed by other words as being superfluous to the meaning of a sentence and the exclamation points that frequently follow them are seen as arrogant. That the rules of English allow interjections to be used as standalone sentences is another reason they are disliked.

Adjectives, adverbs, and prepositions are despised by nouns and verbs that resent being modified; conjunctions are hated for making sentences longer than they should be; and articles are pooh-poohed for being small in number and having to sidle up to nouns to make their presence

34

felt. Long story short, the components of English are crazy and that the language has not been institutionalized can only be ascribed to luck or the fact that if you locked up all its grammatical parts we would have nothing to say because we would not have the means to say it.

So the next time you are in a situation where someone is spouting political talking points in a venomous and hysterical manner, don't get all lathered up about it. It's not that they are biased, low-information nitwits who have rocks in their heads and don't know squat about politics. It's English that's making them talk like fools.

We Need to Stop
Sticking to Our Guns

In 2008, the US Supreme Court ruled that the Second Amendment guarantees the right of individuals to own guns. But that's not all it guarantees. It assures the right to bear *any* sorts of arms, a right sorely needed in a world where weapons development has made rifles and pistols rudimentary armaments of last resort.

If the government sent a mechanized armored brigade to my house to confiscate my computer because they were looking for the evidence I have on my hard drive that Hillary Clinton and AOC fired the fatal shots that killed JFK, I wouldn't have enough firepower with the legally permissible guns I have stowed in my underwear drawer to keep them from busting into my home. If a bunch of M13 gang members equipped with machineguns and rockets purchased on the q.t. from arms dealers in Nicaragua broke into my bank to steal my safety deposit box (which contains, among other things, my marriage certificate, stock certificates, and proof that Kamala Harris is Bill Clinton's love child), the guys guarding the bank would have no chance to stop them, even if the guards were toting AK-47s. If Al-Qaeda loyalists, riding in Humvees and bulletproof personnel carriers, invaded my town to set up shop, there's no way I could defend the burg with lawfully allowed munitions.

The fly in the ointment is the National Firearms Act (NFA), passed in 1934 and amended in 1968, that pertains to machineguns, sawed-off shotguns and rifles, and "destructive devices"—grenades, mortars, rocket launchers, large projectiles, and other heavy stuff. Acquiring these weapons is subject to prior approval by the Attorney General, and federal registration is required for possession. Clearly, with these repressive and unconstitutional restraints, the government is meddling where they have no statutory right to intrude.

The Second Amendment says, "the right of the people to keep and bear arms, shall not be infringed." The Founding Fathers did not specifically define "arms" but I am sure these Enlightenment thinkers knew what were considered arms in the 1700s would evolve over the years. Back then people defended themselves with muskets, long rifles, knives, bayonets, axes, swords, sabers, and pole weapons. If you could afford a cannon you could get one but cannons were tough to transport and loading them was a pain in the ass. You slew as best you could, though by present standards the ways our Revolutionary forbears knocked off people was incredibly cumbersome and woefully inefficient.

George Washington would have killed to get his hands on an M777 howitzer, an M1 Abrams tank, a belt-fed M240 machinegun, an M67 fragmentation grenade, or a tactical nuclear weapon. But all he had to off the Redcoats with was the primitive ordnance extant in the 18th century. Fortunately, we live in the 21st century. The weapons I mentioned at the beginning of this paragraph, if they were made legal for all Americans to own, would make a real difference in the fight against the thugs and brigands that are around now—banditti like the trillions of illegal aliens who are sneaking into our country through its undefended southern border to rape, pillage and wreak

37

havoc in the land; the billions of inner-city criminals who are robbing, rioting, and roaming wild on the streets of our nation's inner cities; and the millions of reformist government bureaucrats that can show up at your door at any hour of the day or night and make outrageous demands on your liberty just because they are bullies and feel like it.

The NRA (National Reprobates Association) needs to get cracking on expanding the kinds of weapons people can legally own. The lawfully sanctioned firearms in the mix today may be okay for killing individuals and small-to-mid-sized groups of human beings but they are not the über killing machines these violent times demand. Such weapons are currently reserved for the US military, which is a shame because if the good people of America could possess advanced military-grade armaments that are currently barred to them, the immigration problem would be solved, crime would be negligible, overseas terrorists would stay the heck away, and the feds would learn to mind their own business and stick to their last.

If you like what I am proposing, please write to your Congressional representative and ask them to support the revocation of the National Firearms Act. All weapons are "destructive" and it's unfair to discriminate amongst them. This is a free country and discrimination is against the law.

Let's make America great again, like it was before gun regulations and a stripped-down interpretation of the Second Amendment put a damper on our ability to defend ourselves. Let's overturn the NFA and get that ability back. It's never to late to do the right thing, which is to allow individuals the right to possess bazookas, stingers, javelin anti-tank weapons, and other equally powerful munitions. The time has long since gone for people's only option to be "stick to your guns."

Boots Without Feet on the Ground

There's not much risk of American military casualties when we fire cruise missiles from ships and drop bombs from planes in our efforts to fight evil overseas. The problem comes when we put boots on the ground, as soldiers in hostile territory are more likely to be killed or injured than sailors or pilots who operate from a distance. Putting boots without feet on the ground solves that problem. Here's how to do it.

Boots would be loaded onto US Air Force planes and dropped over enemy terrain. This would enable us to tell the world that we were serious about our military intentions, as we had boots on the ground. We could also claim we were sending humanitarian aid to the country we were showering shoes on since the locals could use the boots as footwear.

Would women in the countries we were shoe-bombing wear those boots? They would if we dropped some that were stylish, and had cool colors. And we could gift-wrap them so the men who retrieved those boots could give them to their wives and girlfriends as presents, a gesture that would win the men affection from their consorts and America affection from the men, as we had made their largesse possible.

If a pair of boots did not fit they could be exchanged for ones that did. The only stipulation would be that the boots would need to be swapped at US-built department stores, which we would construct in the country we were dropping boots on once things got resolved there. This would make the rebels on our side even more aggressive in their fighting, as who wants to wear boots that hurt your feet.

Where would these boots be manufactured? Well, definitely not in China because if they were made in The People's Republic the Chinese would be able to say they had boots on the ground. They would be produced in the good old USA, which would be a plus for the American economy.

And here's another benefit. Having only footwear on the ground means once the fighting was over we would be able to maintain a perpetual presence in the land our shoes were in without any physical risk to our men and women in uniform. All done on a shoestring budget!

Is "boots without feet on the ground" an out-of-the-box solution to keeping American casualties down and American commerce up in places we decide to militarily intervene in? It certainly is. It's an out-of-the-shoebox solution!

To Be or Not to Be

The Supreme Court judges who voted to abolish *Roe v Wade* advanced a number of arguments that supported their decision. These arguments were fine as far as they went but they weren't the best arguments for overturning *Roe*. The top arguments, presented in the form of replies to misleading pro-choice arguments, appear below.

Misleading Argument #1
The Supreme Court in 1972 declared abortion to be a "fundamental right" protected by the Constitution.

My Reply
That was a stupid declaration made by stupid judges who haven't read the Constitution. The first amendment to that document guarantees everyone the right to free speech, a right you can't enjoy unless you make it out of the womb. The same logic applies to the second amendment, which guarantees the right to bear arms. Ditto all the other amendments and the rights they talk about. You can be sure the Republican-appointed justices who currently serve on the Supreme Court have read the Constitution and understand this argument so even though they didn't mention it in their majority opinion, those in the know say it was on all their minds.

Misleading Argument #2
The Bible says nothing about abortion so it is not a sin in the religious sense of the word.

My Reply

That abortion is a sin is spelled out clearly in the Pat Robertson rendering of the King James Bible, which says in the Book of Mel Gibson 1:8: "a woman who terminates a pregnancy because she feels she has a right to do so is in league with the devil who is probably taking her to bars and clubs and putting lewd thoughts in her head that wouldn't be there if she cohabitated with men who correctly believe that women are bone of their bones, flesh of their flesh, good to look at, and vital for keeping the house clean."

Misleading Argument #3

Personhood begins after a fetus becomes "viable" (able to survive outside the womb) or after birth, not at conception.

My Reply

Scientists who have studied this matter at Bible colleges and conservative think tanks all across the country have determined that human life begins at conception and sometimes even earlier than that. How much earlier is still being investigated but best guesses are sometime between the start of the production of a sperm cell, the development of an unfertilized egg, and whatever day it was when God created Adam.

Misleading Argument #4

Reproductive choice empowers women by giving them control over their own bodies.

My Reply

In America, bodily empowerment comes with limits. For example, men in the US military obey orders all day long telling them what to do with their bodies. The Selective Service System requires males 18-25 to register their bodies for possible conscription. Dudes who go to strip clubs and act fresh with the strippers get their bodies thrown to the curb. The fact is, God is in control of all our bodies and, as any preacher worth his salt will tell you, the Lord wants women to use their bodies to have children.

Live Fast, Die Young

The healthcare system in this country is broken and everyone says something should be done about it. The question is what. Some answers are as follows:

Early to Bed, Early to Rise, Makes a Man Healthy, Wealthy, and Wise

This notion worked for Benjamin Franklin, who died at the age of 84 (40 years beyond the average lifespan of that time), and it can work for you. There's no reason to stay up late. TV shows after ten can be recorded, drinking can be done in the early hours of the evening, and people can live without nighttime snacks. And getting up early isn't hard if you have something to look forward to, like taking care of yourself so you will live to be 120, and have a foghorn attached to your alarm clock. Sweet dreams and good health, my friend.

Become a Doctor

These days, it is not unusual to wait for hours at a doctor's office before being seen. And when you finally do get seen, chances are the doctor won't spend much time listening to your concerns and when you leave their office it will probably be with a prescription rather than a hefty supply of samples. Become a doctor and these problems disappear.

As a doctor you will be able to see yourself immediately, spend as much time as you like talking to yourself about your health issues, and obtain all the drugs you need for nothing. Moreover, with MD license plates you will be able to park your car in restricted spaces when you are out having dinner, attending a show, or visiting friends. And you will have job security. With such great benefits, it's amazing everyone doesn't apply to medical school.

Join the Military

If you join the military, besides receiving free room, board, and a cool looking uniform you'll get your healthcare gratis. This means you won't have to waste time filling out insurance questionnaires if you get sick, or shot. As to that latter prospect, battlefield medicine has vastly improved over the years. Nowadays, if you suffer a combat injury, you'll probably only be maimed or disfigured rather than killed. But the armed forces are not for everyone. If loud noises or the sight of blood puts you off you may want to consider the next suggestion.

Live Fast, Die Young

Do you remember Marilyn Monroe, John Belushi, and James Dean? These famous and talented actors lived fast and died young. No lengthy hospital stays and long-term illnesses for this bunch. A suicide, an overdose, and a car crash, then they were gone. But when they were alive, Monroe, Belushi, and Dean had a ball—all-night parties, loads of booze, out-of-control sex—you name it, they did it. And because they were young they could still get up and go to work the next day.

These entertainers helped society by dying in their prime, as the medical care they would have received had they lived for many years could be given to others. And the government saved on paying them social security. If you are a person who enjoys living life to the max, the live-fast-die-young approach could be perfect for you. But if you choose this option, please do the rest of us a favor. When you're out on the town raising hell and running wild, try not to kill anyone else with your fast living!

Privatizing Schools for Fun and Profit

Lots of studies show private schools are no better than public ones. But many people believe the opposite is true and that belief has created big opportunities for those who want to open private schools. If you are one of these people, here is some advice to help you get started.

You will need to hire teachers, which shouldn't be a problem if the hiring bar is set at the right level. The level I recommend is anyone who has gone to school. This will provide a hiring pool of nearly everybody in the country. If you want to lower the bar a bit, offer the job to anyone with a pulse.

In terms of salary, use the following formula: add the number of years a person has attended school to the person's age, divide by the square root of four, subtract the number of fish there are in the sea, and multiply by one. The result will be a negative integer, which means your employees will have to pay you for the privilege of working. If a prospective hire objects to this arrangement offer them fifty cents an hour above the federal minimum wage. If they still object, offer them fifty cents less.

Recruiting students should be easy if you pay them, and you won't have to pay them much since they're getting nothing from the public schools. But make sure you pay them less than their teachers because if you don't, the teachers will quit and enroll as students in your school. Have the children clean the school as part of their stipend.

There are tons of ways to conserve on food costs. The best way is to have kids bring meals from home. If this is not practical, have the children grow vegetables, milk cows, and raise beef cattle in the schoolyard. If anybody objects to having the kids do these things just say such activities follow John Dewey's philosophy of education: "learning by doing."

To save on transportation costs, ask parents to take their kids to school. In cases where this is not possible, have bicycles available for transport and rent them to the youngsters. Children too young to bike can be picked up by older students and placed in the baskets of their bicycles. And here's a bonus: because biking is such great exercise you won't need to employ Phys. Ed. instructors for the older students.

Your charges will have to take standardized tests and your success, and theirs, will be determined by how well they do on them. To ensure they do well, tell the teachers to teach to the tests; and if they are allowed to grade the exams instruct them to change incorrect answers to correct ones. If the teachers haven't taught the kids well enough so they could achieve high marks on their own they owe this form of help to the children.

Over 90% of startups fail, so don't be hard on yourself if your school goes bust. Your students can always go back to public school and your teachers can find jobs at Walmart or Costco. The important thing is you gave it a try. You tried to make a buck off the kids, scam your staff, and cheat the system. That's a perfect formula to use if after this experience you decide to go into the daycare business.

Disloyal? I Don't Think So!

The patriotic Americans who stormed the Capitol on January 6th did so because Congress was about to ratify the results of a presidential election where millions of illegal immigrants had mailed in votes from their vacation homes by the fields where they worked and millions of would-be Trump voters were forced to stay in their houses by knife-wielding members of Antifa who tied them to their beds. And how about the fact that one man voted 800,000 times for Joe Biden and that Donald Trump's name was not on the ballot in Arizona, Pennsylvania, Michigan, and Georgia.

What were these patriots supposed to do? Accept court verdicts from around the country saying there was no widespread voter fraud? Accept election results that were certified by each state as accurate? Accept the fact that Joe Biden won the popular and electoral vote for president? I don't think so! This is America, where the facts are what you say they are and if you can get enough people to agree with you, you can become president.

Congress was going to do the unimaginable on January 6th, declare the winner of the electoral vote would become president of the United States on January 20th. But what's up with that! Just because you win the electoral vote doesn't mean you become president. The original, hand-written Constitution had a secret provision in it that said the loser of the electoral vote, if he is an incumbent and doing a great job, can remain in office as long as he can convince his base that the election he ran in was rigged and that the deep state is out to get white people. That's what happened here!

The truth is, Donald Trump should have been declared the winner of the 2020 presidential election in October 2020 and Joe Biden should have gone home to Delaware to play with his grandchildren. But that was not going to happen. Rather, the US Congress was going to proclaim that a one-hundred-ten-year-old leftist pawn with delusions of grandeur and his evil black queen were going to become president and vice president of the United States.

President Trump tried to right this injustice by calling for a rally of his supporters, people worthy of the Presidential Medal of Freedom and weekend discount rates at the Trump International Hotel in Washington, DC. These people, perhaps best represented by groups such as the Proud Boys, Oath Keepers, and Three Percenters, wanted to stop the steal and save American democracy from degenerating into a play-it-by-the-rules operation.

On the morning of January 6th, an army of liberty lovers got together peacefully on the Ellipse Grounds in Washington DC where they heard our wonderful president tell them "if you don't fight like hell, you're not going to have a country any more." In response, they marched to the Capitol and occupied the Halls of Congress on behalf of the American people. This led to fake outrage by some Republican legislators, who, because a few individuals died in the attack and some property was damaged, condemned the great Americans who sacked America's swamp-filled seat of government. But these turncoat

Republican lawmakers should have focused their wrath on the true villains: people who voted for Joe Biden and Kamala Harris—two Marxist politicians who want everyone to have affordable health care, a decent education, and a worry-free retirement.

Every Republican legislator should have praised the brave men and women who took the law into their own hands and tried to show the nation that spite makes right, white makes right, and the right is right about everything. That's been the Republican playbook since the 1990s because when a party relies on a minority of voters, and those voters don't want their number to expand, it's the absolute right thing to do.

Photograph By Katherine Liepe-Levinson

PART 2: SEMANTIC ANTICS

Dinner at the Woke Street Café

When I entered the Woke Street Café—a hip new restaurant that caters to the woke, those wanting to be woke, and individuals curious about the idea of "wokeness"—I tried to check my privilege at the door but was told unless I agreed to sign up to receive emails from Bernie Sanders, Elizabeth Warren, and members of the squad it would not be accepted. I thought that fair so I clicked yes to that request when it came up on my cellphone and was handed a status tag by the restaurant's status attendant. I was then taken to my table, which was adorned with a plain, inoffensive tablecloth; politically correct cutlery, a recycled paper napkin, a list of grievances from people who have reached adulthood in the second decade of the 21st century, and a pamphlet on the merits of socialism.

A waitperson brought me a menu and asked if I'd care to order a drink. I said I would and requested he recommend something. He said the Cuba Libre was a beverage he was partial to, as he hailed from Cuba and was a proud Hispanic who had married a Latina who was born in Brazil so she could not be called an Hispanic because, according to the US census bureau, people of Portuguese or Brazilian descent are not considered Hispanic but she didn't care because the majority of Latino-Americans prefer to identify with their families' country of origin. I ordered the Cuba Libre.

While sipping my libation I looked over the choices on the menu, which included *cisgender salad* (a salad whose gender identity was assigned when it was prepared in the kitchen), *biologically challenged potatoes* (tubers grown in harsh

56

conditions on the steppes of Russia), and *gluten-free-range vegan salmon* (salmon raised on vegetables without gluten in cage-free, filtered-water spawning grounds). I decided to go with a simple inclusive pasta that contained ziti, spaghetti, rigatoni, linguini, fettuccini, cannelloni, macaroni, rotini, and penne served with a light sprinkling of garlic and olive oil and garnished with a disclaimer saying that the restaurant does not discount the nutritional importance of red and white sauce nor the inherent value of pappardelle, orecchiette, tagliatelle, and all other marginalized pastas. To accompany my entrée I ordered a non-binary vegetable/fruit dish that had in it cucumbers, pumpkins, tomatoes, and ten other "vegetables" that, botanically speaking, could be considered fruits. For dessert I ordered a BDS hot fudge sundae that featured chocolate sauce from the West Bank and nuts and rockets from Gaza.

While eating my meal I received a text from an LGBTQIAGNC neighbor who wanted to know if I was confused when they referred to themselves as "they," which everyone in the wokerati knows is a singular, non-binary, gender-neutral, reflexive pronoun used by individuals who are sensitive to the way our culture limits gender identification. I replied I was sure I would get used to the notion that "they" was an emerging pronoun that referred to a person who rejected the traditional binary "he" or "she." They texted back they were happy I felt that way and I was happy they were happy and I felt even happier when they said they had recently met a very nice person whose individual gender was unknown and they were taking themselves to Starbucks for a couple of double espressos and some indigenous non-gendered pound cake.

After I finished my dinner I signaled for the check. When I received it I noticed an overcharge and told that to my server who rather than being apologetic for the error said, "OK, boomer, I'll get you another check." When I said his reference to my generational cohort seemed somewhat dismissive he replied, "Baby boomers have destroyed the economy and don't care about the future so it's hard not to feel a tad micro-aggressive when I serve an older, privileged person like yourself."

Not wanting to get into an argument with the waitron, or be perceived as waiterphobic or systemically oppressive, I told the soup juggler to forget about giving me another check and that I would simply pay the full amount. I also said he might want to consider taking a course in customer relations and give trigger warnings when he attacked people. Sadly, my gestures of good will were not taken by the tray trotter in the spirit I had intended and I was called a victim-blaming, socially misaligned, selectively perceptive, charm-free, negative-attention-getting, dysfunctional earth child, to which I responded, "Sticks and stones may break my bones but words can really harm me, if you are woke and not a joke you'll find a safe space for me."

The safe space turned out to be my car, which I drove home in feeling a bit shaken but fully awakened to the idea that there is a lot about the woke generation and its lingo that I don't understand and that, in the interests of being less horizontally challenged and more sustainably fit, I probably should have just ordered the cisgender salad and nixed the dessert.

Melancholia and Polemius

Melancholia was the daughter of Polemius, the God of Adhesives, and Tipsy, the Goddess of Fermented Grape Juice. She was the offspring of an unhappy union, for when she was a babe she was glued to her highchair by her father who then struck her mother with an anvil and turned himself into a roll of Scotch tape to avoid the wrath of Zeus. But Zeus was not so easily deceived and he fired a bolt of lightning as big as the Empire State Building at the disguised Polemius, which caused Polemius to melt into a puddle of plastic that was licked up by Cerberus, the three-headed dog of the underworld.

Melancholia found herself abandoned and stuck in a place she wanted no part of and if it had not been for Eucalyptus, the Goddess of air fresheners and medicinal teas, and her son Maalox, the God of regularity, she would have wound up with Eurydice in Hadestown. But the gods had other things planned for Melancholia and before you could say "what the hell is this story all about" she was swept into the sky by a strong north wind that had been sent by Fistula, the God of abnormal connections, who desired her in a licentious sort of way.

While all this was happening, Borax, the God of household cleaners and laundry detergent boosters, and his wife Clorox, the Goddess of liquid bleach, were conspiring with Sangria, the Goddess of wine punches popular with foreign tourists visiting Spain, to kidnap Melancholia and hold her for ransom. Unfortunately for them, Tumult, the God of chaos, and Kardashia, the Goddess of reality TV programs, discovered the plot and told Fistula about what Borax, Clorox, and Sangria were planning.

Fistula asked his nephew Hermes, the messenger God of fine leather and silk products, and his niece Hera, a very powerful Goddess known mostly for her jealousy and tight designer dresses, to help him stop Tumult and Kardashia from absconding with Melancholia. They agreed to assist him and called on Potholus, the God of ruined roads, to create fissures on the path that Tumult and Kardashia would have to take to get to Melancholia, who, after being swept up to the sky, had landed on a beach in Carmel, California where she was living with Hephaestus, the God of names incredibly difficult to spell and pronounce.

Meantime, Zeus was having second thoughts about his decision to liquefy Polemius. So he called on Calypso, the Goddess-nymph of the mythical island of Gilligan, who advised him to see her cousin Cronos, the God of time and six-letter words not legal in Scrabble, and ask him if he would set his clocks back to before the hour when Zeus threw his thunderbolt at Polemius.

Cronos agreed to Zeus's request and set his timepieces back to even earlier than Zeus asked him to, which enabled Zeus to have his granduncle Hypnos, the God of hocus-pocus, hypnotize Polemius into a state of perfect composure. With Polemius zoned out, Tipsy and Melancholia were spared the terrible fates that befell them when this tale began.

And this is why we must always hope that the gods are with us when it comes to granting do-overs and maintaining good family relations and that they will take pity on us if we decide to paste our children to their seats and/or do away with our spouses.

Holiday Newsletter

Dear Friends:

This was a banner year for our family. I published five books that made the *New York Times* bestseller list, finished first in the New York City Marathon, was awarded a Genius Grant from the MacArthur Foundation and, as luck would have it, won the grand prize in the New York State Lottery. Kathy was given the Hasselblad Award (considered the most prestigious in the world) for her world-class photography, made the *Forbes* list of the "One Hundred Most Powerful Businesswomen in the World," won the Mrs. America beauty contest, and discovered a cure for osteopordisis (a disease that occurs when you get dissed so hard your bones break down).

Our two cats also had a wonderful 365 days. Max, our eldest, was accepted to Tufts Medical School, where he will be studying to become a radiologist—Max just loves doing CAT scans. He also won plaudits for the excellent valedictory he delivered last June to the graduates of the Dalton School of Fish. Buddy, his younger brother, was awarded the Nobel Prize for Literature for his 900-page novel *Of Mice and Cats*. Buddy was also named NASCAR driver of the year for his dramatic come-from-behind win at the Puss and Boots 500 in Indianapolis. We're very pleased with the accomplishments of both our pets and can't wait to see what new honors will befall our fabulous felines in the next twelve months.

Our surroundings did very well too. The editors of *Money* magazine named our neighborhood "the best place to live on earth," and *Architectural Digest* noted in their is-

61

sue on *Iconic American Houses* that the house we live in is "the most intriguing and beautiful house in the United States." We're extremely proud of our neighborhood, our house, and ourselves, as we clearly made an outstanding choice to live where we do.

As far as our hopes and wishes for next year, we hope more glory falls upon us and we wish it would be evenly spread out—that way we'll always have something to celebrate. We also hope that Steven Spielberg will come through on his promise to make a movie from the screenplay we sent him (you know which one it is, Steven) and that the President will honor the verbal commitment he gave us at the White House that if a Supreme Court position opens up, one of us can have it.

Peace on earth, goodwill to all, and remember no matter how well you do in the coming year, it won't compare to all the honors and accolades we'll be getting.

All best,
Us and the cats

At the End of the Day
There's Another...Cliché

At the end of the day, the day is over. That's the God's honest truth. If you want a longer day get up at the crack of dawn. Early to bed, early to rise, makes a man healthy, wealthy, and wise.

Some people strut their stuff, line their ducks up in a row, step into the sunshine, and have the time of their lives. Well gather ye rosebuds while ye may but the world is no one's oyster. Life's a long, hard slog and in the end we all have to pay the piper.

Other people go through existence with their backs against the wall, always at loose ends, thinking what doesn't kill them makes them stronger. To these folks, life's a bitch and then you marry one. Hey, I'm not going to bury my head in the sand and say life's a bowl of cherries, but the show must go on, the game's worth the candle, so eat, drink, and be merry.

But don't sink your teeth into too much food. Quit while you're ahead. That's the best way to keep oneself fit as a fiddle. While it's okay to let yourself go now and again, if you eat like a horse and drink like a fish you can bet your bottom dollar you'll be pushing up daisies sooner rather than later.

Speaking of flowers, I know a place where, come hell or high water, cheap blossoms are there for the asking. You can have them for a song. If you think I'm pulling your chain, call my bluff and check the joint out.

To keep the ball rolling, I also know a place where clothing can be bought on the cheap. It's a snap to get to, even for people who can't find their way out of a paper bag and are dumber than a box of rocks. And the service there is to die for. The employees don't have a take-it-or-leave-it attitude. They'll go the extra mile for you.

Like every Tom, Dick, and Harry, I want to be served toot suite when I go shopping. It drives me up a wall when I enter a store and the salesclerks are just chewing the fat with each other and taking up space. Hey, I'm busier than a ten-peckered dog in a hydrant factory. I don't have time to screw around.

And lots of salespeople don't know diddlysquat. It seems every time I ask a salesperson about a product they say, "It's the greatest thing since sliced bread." But I guess I should count my blessings. I could be told, "I'm busy right now, I'll get back to you in a jiff," and then the person telling me that takes a powder and I don't see hide nor hare of them.

I yearn for the good old days, when you didn't have to fight tooth and nail to be waited on and all was right with the world. But that era has come and gone. Now it's every man for himself, rob Peter to pay Paul, do whatever tickles your pickle.

I hope you don't think I'm like a time bomb waiting to explode. I'm not. I can take it or leave it, ride the tide, go with the flow. But lately I've been up to my neck in alligators and that's made it difficult for me to maintain an even keel. Still, my Momma didn't raise no fool and I want to age gracefully, so I'm going to try to stay cool. Better to keep your shirt on and not get bent out of shape, because you don't have to be a rocket scientist or the smartest guy in the room to know if you let people get under your skin, sure as you're born you'll get caught by the shorthairs.

Three Words Max

Twitter has done a good job limiting content in electronic interactions to 280 characters. But that number can be improved on. I have created a cyber-message service that restricts electronic exchanges to a maximum of just three words. Here are a few examples of what such exchanges might look like.

A Three-Word Electronic Exchange between a Husband and Wife

Having an affair
  With whom?
My secretary Sally
  Why?
Mid-life crisis
  You love her?
Don't think so
  Don't think so?
That's right
  You bastard!
You sound angry
  I am angry
That's understandable
  I hate you

Don't get emotional
   Screw you
Screw you too
   Want a divorce
Okay by me
   Fantastic!
Nice knowing you
   Likewise, I'm sure

A Three-Word Electronic Exchange between Romeo and Juliet

O, Romeo, Romeo!
   O sweet Juliet
Wherefore art thou?
   In the kitchen
What you doing?
   Boiling eggs
Make mine soft
   Like your lips
Ye flatter me
   Pray, I don't
Yea you do
   Maybe a little
Stupid answer

67

Don't get emotional
Say something clever
    I'm fortune's fool
That's pretty good
    I love you
Even better
    Got to go
Parting's such sorrow
    Don't feel badly
Why not?
    Be back tomorrow

A Three-Word Electronic Exchange between a Caller to a Suicide Hotline and a Hotline Receptionist

Want to die
    Tell me more
My life sucks
    You sound depressed
I am depressed
    Tried anti-depressants?
Don't like medicine
    How about psychotherapy?
Don't like psychologists
    Positive thinking?

68

Are you nuts!

 Don't get emotional

I'm suicidal dummy

 Lighten up Bud

Who's Bud?

 You

My name's Joe

 Ease up Joe

Don't know how

 Knock knock

Who's there?

 Yule

Yule who?

 Yule never know!

That's funny

 Laughter's good medicine

I'm feeling better

 Great!

You saved me

 Got another call

(New Caller)

Want to die

(Receptionist)

 Knock knock

69

A Few New Mental Disorders

The *Diagnostic and Statistical Manual of Mental Disorders* (*DSM*), the guidebook widely used by clinicians and psychiatrists in the United States, is currently being revised, which means a comprehensive literature review, analyses of data sets, and field trials on the most substantial or controversial proposals. What's missing in this process is input from members of the public on possible new mental disorders and their treatments. That input should be solicited and if it is I suggest the following four mental disorders worthy of *DSM* inclusion.

Paying Attention Disorder (PAD)

Paying Attention Disorder is a psychological condition that involves being attentive to whomever or whatever one is involved with. It can be seen in individuals who try to engage others in meaningful discussion rather than speak on their cell phones, text, or tweet during conversations. These people genuinely attempt to talk and listen to the individuals around them. Typically, their efforts are ignored because paying attention to others during person-to-person exchanges is a useless artifact from the pre-internet era.

To overcome PAD, the patient should watch TV talk shows and listen to political debates. Working for a telecommunications company is also recommended, as telecom employees are specially trained to never pay attention to anyone. Alternatively, the patient can try to find employment as a customer-relations representative for a cable company or major American airline.

70

Single Personality Disorder (SPD)

To meet the ongoing challenges and changing conditions that characterize today's hectic, fast-paced world, one has to be pliant and be able to reinvent oneself. That's a lot easier to do if you have multiple personalities. If you have just one it is almost impossible.

Imagine you are a shy, humorless person with a single personality who is working as a reference librarian and the library you work for shuts down. You've got bills to pay and you need to find a job quickly but the only employment available in town is doing standup at Sam's Cabaret and Comedy Club. Sadly, you won't make much money if Sam hires you because reciting numbers from the Dewey Decimal System just isn't that funny.

To gain additional personalities, the patient should be encouraged to watch movies and adopt the personas of the various characters appearing on the screen. Another strategy the patient can use is to ask a person with multiple personalities if he or she would be willing to sell a few of them. Finally, the patient can buy a lotto ticket and hope they win the grand prize. If that happens the patient can behave however they like.

Lack of Narcissism Personality Disorder (LNPD)

"Narcissistic personality disorder" is listed as a mental condition in the *DSM*. But this categorization is no longer valid, as recent studies indicate that those who have an exaggerated sense of their own importance are the rule in American society. The problem is lack of narcissism, which, to put a label on it, could be classified as Lack of Narcissism Personality Disorder (LNPD).

To treat LNPD, advise the patient to go to Bloomingdale's with a credit card and say to the salespeople there, "I want to look better than everyone else on the planet. Can you help me to do that?" The *oohs* and *ahs* that the patient will receive from the fawning sales staff as he or she buys loads of expensive clothing and accouterments should convince them that they're the cat's meow. Coaching on how to dominate conversations and blame others when you make a mistake can be useful adjuncts in developing an outsized sense of self-importance.

Talk Radio Addiction (TRA)

Talk Radio Addiction is a compulsion to listen to talk radio programs and then accuse one's spouse and colleagues of being wacky out-of-touch liberals who should leave the country if they think things are so bad. TRA sufferers are fond of conflict and refuse to be swayed by the facts. When they take a stand on something they will normally brook no opposition, however a rant by Sean Hannity or a radical lobotomy may occasionally lead them to reverse an opinion.

TRA is a difficult disease to treat because the patient does not think he is sick. He thinks you are. Diverting the patient's attention can be tried and while he is distracted one can switch the channel to a sports or music station. Over time the patient may develop a liking for one of those forms of entertainment. In some cases, surgery has been successful in opening a person's mind but the procedure is risky and should only be attempted by highly trained specialists who have tremendous patience in dealing with complete and total morons.

Fifty Shades of Green

Driving home with her in his limited-edition onyx-black Bentley Mulliner Bacalar, with its signature 6.0 liter, W12 turbocharged engine that can deliver 650 horsepower and 664 pound-feet, he felt confident things would go well in the bedroom. How could they not? She seemed charmed when they went to Columbus Circle for dinner at Per Se, where they dined on Japanese Hamachi Tartare, Diamond-H Ranch quail breast, Hudson Valley Moulard duck foie gras, prime rib of Elysian Fields farm lamb, and a host of other delectable comestibles. She had laughed at his jokes and praised his wardrobe, which was indeed worthy of acclaim.

That night he had chosen to wear a blue-gray Brioni bespoke suit made from the blends of some of the rarest and most expensive fibers in the world. A shiny black Cartier crocodile and palladium belt lined with 70 small pezzottaite pyramids held up his pants. His shirt was a powder blue, Luigi Borrelli, Sea Island, Shahtoosh, extralong staple, Nepalese cotton number, which he complemented with Bulgari benitoite azure-blue cufflinks and a Stefano Ricci rep tie made of pure Lotus and Mulberry silk, fashioned from 150 grams of jeremejevite with streaks of emerald and demantoid garnets. The shoes he donned were a pair of Tom Ford fire-opal loafers customized by Oscar de la Renta, Christian Loboutin, and Yves St. Laurent.

She was his peer in lavish attire. Her Imperial red, Dita von Teese dirndl dress, made of silk satin, was ornamented with Zari embroidery, 1,000 La Peregrina pearls, and 150,000 Swarovski crystals. It was a stunner, and her Salvatore Ferragamo patent crimson leather, stiletto-heel shoes embellished with rubies, rhinestones, and red beryl were an equal wow. Floral Van Cleef and Arpels ear clips crafted in 18-karat white gold and set with bixbite from the Violet Claim in Utah's WahWahmountains, dangled from her earlobes and her fingers were festooned with rings that featured jadeite, sapphire, alexandrite, musgravite, grandidierite, and painite gemstones. Octavia Ferlinghetti's KissKiss Sapphire and Serendibite lipstick, which she applied from a case adorned with 110 grams of solid 18-carat yellow gold, paved with a rain of 199 diamonds of 2.2 carats, provided the perfect accompaniment to her opulent garb.

When they reached her apartment, she asked him if he would like a drink. He said he wouldn't mind having some Macallan Fine & Rare Vintage Single Malt Scotch, and she replied, "Coming up." While he was sipping his libation, she excused herself to put on something more comfortable and when she returned he could see she had done that. In place of her eveningwear, she was sporting a Karolina Kurkova balconette-style hearts-on-fire fantasy bra, garlanded with 2,000 perfectly cut Enrico Fermi non-radioactive isotopes and a 42-carat emerald brooch at the center, along with a Kiki De Montparnasse enchanted G-string yellow-spinel, beaded-lace thong.

He asked her if it would be okay for him to remove his clothes too, and she nodded in assent. So he stripped down to his Derek Rose pure silk classic-fit boxers and they both climbed onto her Jado Steel Style tanzanite bed that was covered with Charlotte Thomas 1000-thread sheets made of 22-karat gold woven into fabric crafted from the finest merino wool, backed with a silk jacquard, added to high-quality Egyptian cotton. The pillowcases were made of the same material.

She flipped on the TV remote and the show that popped up on the Bang & Olufsen Beovision, 580-pound, 103-inch TV-screen that hung on the opposite wall from the bed was *The Secret Lives of the Super Wealthy*, the sight of which put them both over the edge. After screaming, "That's the way I want to live!" and "You can never be too rich or decked out!" they orgasmed simultaneously and apart from each other.

They cleaned up with some "forget-me-not-flower" Jūnihitoe tissues, which in Japan have been described as "vibrantly dyed, soft, and delicate, with a quality feel and texture of a traditional Washi paper," and a couple of D. Porthault, 65-gram, Egyptian cotton, double-rolled, hand-sewn, scalloped-edged towels. Then, tired from their sexual exertions, they fell asleep in each other's arms, secure in the knowledge that if the stains on the sheets from their climaxes could not be completely removed in the laundry, they could always ask one of their houseboys to order new ones.

Safe Space University

New Student Orientation

Welcome to Safe Space University, an institution of higher learning where you are free to express yourself without fear of being made to feel uncomfortable, unwelcome, or challenged on account of biological sex, race, ethnicity, sexual orientation, gender identify or expression, sports teams you root for, the beer you like, thoughts you have about being special, and a million other things you may worry could hinder your feelings of ease and tranquility on campus—for a list of those things see www.atSSUwehaveyourback.

To ensure your safety in the classroom and on our grounds, you will be given a body cam that will allow you to record teachers, classmates, members of the custodial staff, campus security, the people who work in the dining room, the people behind the register at the bookstore, the school's librarians, townspeople and visitors who may be on campus, and anyone else who makes comments that you feel threaten your worldview and psychological well-being as a person who knows right from wrong, up from down, and a hateful and evilly intentioned argument when they come across one.

When you start recording what you believe are harmful remarks from a particular individual, an alarm will be transmitted to the Office of Hear No Evil See No Evil Speak No Evil (OHNESNESNE), which is located on the second floor of the administration building. The Office is staffed with lawyers, psychologists, harmful-speech investigators, and specially trained dogs that can determine whether a person who is dog whistling is sending out subtly aimed political messages or is simply using a high-pitched whistle to train a dog.

Following receipt of your alarm, someone from the Office of Hear No Evil, et al will be dispatched to where you are recording to help document the injury being done to you. Afterward, that person can help you to sue, cancel, and make sure the perpetrator of your disquiet will never set foot in the hallowed halls or on the peaceful quads of Safe Space University again.

Our teachers have been instructed to provide trigger warnings in their classrooms prior to sharing what might be construed as potentially disturbing content—things like graphic references to topics such as sexual abuse, self-harm, violence, eating disorders, or anything else a plaintiff's lawyer might convince a jury of in attempting to win money from the college on behalf of an aggrieved undergraduate. If you feel in any way discomfited during a lesson by something being taught you are free to put on headphones, go under your desk, and play video games or tweet your friends until the presentation of the offensive material has concluded, at which point your teacher will text you an all clear so you can return to your seat.

It can be disturbing for a person who has been conditioned all their lives to think in certain ways to suddenly be confronted with notions that differ from their own. It can sometimes result in brain damage or PTSD. To help combat such awful possibilities, while you are at SSU you will be housed with students whose political and social views are exactly like yours. This will allow you to make friends more easily and permit you to stay within your citadel of knowledge.

We wish you the best of luck during the next four years as you develop into the wonderful and caring person, persons, or whatever entity you imagine you are developing into. Stay healthy, stay strong, and have the time of your life here knowing that, to quote from our university mission statement and our touch-football team's fight song, "Those who give up essential liberty to obtain a little temporary safety, shall live to fight another day."

Three National Holidays that
Don't Exist and Shouldn't

National Be Civil and Courteous to Others Day

This nation was built on the idea of freedom to speak one's own mind and shout down the other guy. That's what happened when, in response to Patrick Henry telling the Virginia House of Burgesses, "Give me liberty, or give me death," a heckler cried "Why just one option! How about give me death or a bad case of shingles or a week in the stockade or some other terrible punishment." Americans like to tell it like it is, and it is whatever we say it is.

Abraham Lincoln tried to be civil to the South before the Civil War and where did that get him. Woodrow Wilson attempted to be nice to the Germans but that didn't keep them from sinking American ships. Bill Clinton was affable to the Republicans, and they responded by shutting down the government.

It's in our nature as the offspring of revolutionaries to get in each other's faces and hurl insults, invective, and innuendo at the individuals we are speaking with, particularly if they are members of a political party we don't like. We love to air our grievances and knock the opinions of others and if they can't take it, so much the better. We're not fans of listening politely and giving thought to what other people are saying. We think civility is for pussies, which is what we are not. We are Americans. We are pit bulls.

Electronics Fasting Day

I know what you're thinking: we're all are too hooked on the internet and social media to last 24 hours without them. The American people would never agree to stay off Google, Instagram, Facebook, Twitter, and email for an entire day. You're right, of course, and there's more to the tale. Studies done at MIT and Caltech have shown that steering clear of the internet and social media for as little as ten minutes can induce PTSD and panic attacks in many individuals.

Besides posttraumatic stress syndrome and severe anxiety, there would be other repercussions from leaving the virtual world for a day. Feeling bored and with nothing to do, people might binge eat, take drugs, or, God forbid, read a book. Not being on their electronic devices, and as a consequence seeing the faces of folks they live with who they hadn't bothered to look at in a very long time, some individuals might be overwhelmed by the experience of talking to human beings they no longer recognize.

The fact is, Americans don't want to live in the real world. We're all quite happy being alone together in a virtual one filled with Facebook friends, Instagram influencers, and Twitter followers, a world we have all gotten used to where technology rules and people are plugins.

National Do One Thing at a Time Day

America is about multi-tasking. We're a can-do nation that believes the more you can do at once the more you can accomplish. Right now I am at home where I am using my left hand to type an email to my boss, using my right hand to text a colleague, speaking on my cellphone to a friend, listening to a Beethoven piano concerto, doing chair exercises to strengthen my buns, and . . . meditating. Later, at lunch, I plan to simultaneously prepare and eat a meatball sandwich, do the *New York Times Crossword Puzzle*, learn French on my iPad, do chair exercises to strengthen my calves, practice singing exercises that my vocal coach gave me, and do some . . . meditating. I wish I could do more but there are only 48 hours in a day and you have to sleep for some of them.

If I paid attention to each thing I was doing I would barely accomplish anything. I barely do accomplish anything compared to my wife who can do sixteen things at the same time while making a broccoli and cheese omelet for breakfast, getting the kids off to school, returning calls from patients she sees in her medical practice, preparing notes for a poetry class she teaches on Zoom, power washing the outside of our house, and . . . meditating.

Paying attention to things ceased to exist when TV was invented and with all the electronic devices that people are on today, and with research showing that the average human attention span is less than that of a goldfish, I can't imagine we will ever go back to concentrating on anything. And that's a good thing because you only live once so if you have the technology and a little get-up-and-go why not pack a thousand lifetimes into the experience.

Farewell the Three "R"s

The three "R"s—*reading, 'riting,* and *'rithmetic*—were the mainstay of our education system for many years. But they've become outdated and a new model should be put in place. I propose it be the three "I"s—*imaging, interacting through electronics,* and *integer punching.*

The inclusion of *imaging* in the curriculum is based on the notion that, since a picture is worth a thousand words, it makes no sense to use language to communicate thoughts and ideas. Need to write a thousand-word essay—show a drawing. Assigned a term paper—five to ten illustrations should do the trick. Have to deliver a lecture—hold up a few photos.

Images have a big advantage over words as they can be grasped right away. For example, why spend weeks reading books and articles to learn about World War II when you can cut to the chase in two hours and forty-nine minutes by watching *Saving Private Ryan.* Want to get the gist of *War and Peace?* Check out the TV mini-series. It's far less time consuming and much easier to follow than the book.

Images appeal to our emotions more viscerally than language does and that's a huge plus because, as Mark Zuckerberg can tell you, feeling trumps thought when it comes to understanding the world. Thinking takes work, a four-letter word not fit for mixed company.

To implement image education in school, reading teachers would be phased out and photography and video instructors phased in; the SAT exam would include a section requiring drawn responses to pictures; and comic books would replace textbooks. Imaging would put our nation in a much better position to meet the educational challenges of the new millennium because in a world where TV programs and videos are key sources of information, it's not what you know, it's what you can show.

Interacting through electronics is the second leg of the three-I model. Before texting and emailing, people frequently connected with each other by writing letters, which meant you had to know something about the rules of grammar, usage, and correct spelling. But that's no longer the case, as is shown in the following poem.

The Spelling Checker

Eye halve a spelling checker
It came with my pea sea
It plainly marks four my revue
Miss steaks eye kin knot sea.
Eye strike a key and type a word
And weight four it two say
Weather eye am write oar wrong
It shows me strait a weigh.

Formal writing should be tossed from the curriculum and electronic inscription, which includes the use of chat speak (lol, btw, omg) and emoticons, should take its place. Communicating electronically is much cooler and way more efficient in connecting with others than using boring Standard English—to wit: "When I watched the sun in all its magnificent and resplendent glory rise up over the mountains this morning, I felt intensely grateful and over-joyed to be alive" versus "OMG, Sunrise ☺!"

The last of the three "I"s, *integer punching*, involves using a calculator to do arithmetic computations. The process is easy to learn and does away with having to master addition, subtraction, multiplication, and division. Once students get the hang of it they can forget about math and shift their focus to what really counts like trying to become an influencer, trolling people on social media, and playing video games.

Imaging, interacting through electronics, and *integer punching*—for state-of-the-art education in the twenty-first century, the "I"s have it!

It's Five O'Clock Somewhere

Everyone likes Happy Hour with its cheap drinks, free appetizers, and the opportunity it provides to socialize with friends and associates. But the label is kind of boring and does not consider specific motivations that might draw people to attend what has become an iconic American ritual. Here are four new ways to market that ritual.

Tribal Loyalty Hour

We live in a country consumed by the idea that the groups we belong to are superior to or being victimized by the groups we don't belong to. This leads us to hate those other groups for taking up space in the world. To find solace, some people tune in to radio and TV talk shows with hosts who say terrible things about the groups they despise. Other people tweet, and even re-tweet, horrible stuff about the groups they loathe. But loathing by one's lonesome is not as much fun or psychologically reinforcing as being with others who share one's antipathies.

And so tribal loyalty hour, a stretch in the late afternoon or early evening where you can hunker down with fellow malcontents and over cut-rate drinks and food, rag on all the groups you and they can't stand. Doing this can be therapeutic and cleanse a person of the ridiculous desire to see individuals as individuals rather than as parts of socially determined units. If tribal loyalty hour had a mantra it might go something like this: "Time is never wasted when you're wasted with friends and acquaintances who want to verbally waste everyone in groups not like theirs."

Schadenfreude Hour

There is a word for the satisfaction you get when your ex's house burns down or something bad happens to a Kardashian. It is *Schadenfreude*, a German-derived word for the happiness obtained from the misery of others, the idea of which is part of the human condition: The French speak of *joie maligne*, malicious enjoyment derived from other people's angst. In Danish it is labeled *skadefryd*; in Slovak škodoradost; in Mandarin *xìng-zāi-lè-huò*; and in Russian, *zloradstvo*. The Japanese have a saying "The misfortune of others tastes like honey." For the Melanesians who live on the Nissan Atoll in Papua New Guinea, it is *banbanam*.

There is no better way to celebrate other people's grief and bad luck than gathering together in the late afternoon or early evening and toasting to their misfortunes. It's happy hour on steroids.

Stupid Hour

Stupid Hour goes right to the heart of what drinking is all about, namely permission to suspend your reason and act like a jerk. If you behave badly you can blame it on the alcohol, which, since it's a liquid without a solid brain, can't testify in its own defense. Anyway, if everyone is drinking and behaving badly, it's not about defense. It's about offense, specifically how offensive you can be.

Life is often not easy and even when it is we still have to be alert and guard against the slings and arrows of outrageous fortune. No one can be on guard 24/7. Sometimes we just want to let our hair down and act silly. And that means having a little drinkypoo or, if drinks are on

86

sale, maybe a few little drinkypoos, which on a cost per drink basis makes ordering multiple drinks a sensible idea. But sense is beside the point of Stupid Hour, a time when people can cry into their beer knowing if their tears make their beer taste bad they can always order another for half price.

Bitching Hour

A great way to bond with people is to join them in generalized complaining. That has been true since the time of Adam and Eve, when each of those sinners crabbed to the other about having to exit a carefree existence in heaven for a hardscrabble life on Earth. Bellyaching is part of humankind's emotional DNA, like rooting for a local sports team that has no chance of winning or bawling like a baby when you get your cable bill.

Enter Bitching Hour, the perfect occasion for having people meet and over low-cost libations and snacks gripe to each other about how their partner does not understand them, how they hate their jobs, how they wish they were someone else, and how even if they were someone else they wouldn't be happy. Whining and whiskey, carping and cocktails, moaning and merlot: perfect mixtures for promoting the camaraderie that comes from guzzling and grousing alongside a gaggle of grumbling friends.

A Millennial's Take on Dickens

It was sort of the best of times, it was kind of the worst of times, it was like the age of wisdom, it appeared to be the age of foolishness, it seemed the epoch of belief, it looked meh with respect to incredulity, it was man-crush Monday, it was woman-crush Wednesday, it was arguably the spring of hope, it was for all intents and purposes the winter of despair, we had lots of things before us, we had almost nothing before us, we were all going more or less to heaven, we were all trying to Netflix and chill—in short, the period was somewhat like the present one where some of the most humble-bragging trolls were able to foment a revolution and do a fair amount of canceling and shade throwing in a woke kind of way without a fear of adulting or a fear of missing out.

Death by Idiom

(A two-character tragedy)

Setting

Two guys talking to each other in a room

JOE

Can I be frank with you about Jack?

JIM

Certainly, but I want to be Jed.

JOE

Who's Jed?

JIM

A person I invented.

JOE

Why would you invent someone?

JIM

Because if you can be Frank when you talk to me I don't see why I can't be someone else when I talk to you.

JOE

I'm not trying to be another person. When I said, "Can I be frank with you" I was only trying to convey that I wanted to be completely honest with you.

89

JIM

So, if you *don't* say "Can I be frank with you" are you lying to me?

JOE

Of course not. To be honest with you, I always try to be honest with you.

JIM

Why are you doubling down on honesty?

JOE

I'm not doubling down on honesty and, to be candid, I don't know why you'd think I was. Let me put it this way, "To tell you the truth, I tell you the truth."

JIM

All this truth telling is making me sick.

JOE

That's silly. Truth be told, I'm simply a person who doesn't like to beat around the bush.

JIM

Except for hunters, landscapers, and maybe Al Gore, no one likes beating around bushes. You're a pretty weird guy, Joe.

JOE

I'd say I'm a guy who likes to lay it on the line.

JIM

Well I'm a guy who likes to avoid lines. I think you have a problem speaking plainly and directly.

JOE

How about this for plain speaking: when I communicate with people I am open and aboveboard. It makes me sad that you're so skeptical and suspicious, Jim.

JIM

I think anybody would be suspicious of a person talking about being above an imaginary board. Would the board whack you for telling a falsehood if you slipped below it? Stop giving me gobbledygook.

JOE

I'm not giving you gobbledygook. I'm giving you the real deal.

JIM

So now we're playing cards! What kind of moron resorts to games of chance to convince another person of their honesty!

JOE

Would you rather I say I'm giving you the *real truth*? Do you like that better?

JIM

No! Is there a difference between "real truth" and "phony truth?" Truth is truth.

JOE

That's true, which is why as someone who reveres and cherishes verisimilitude I always speak straight from the shoulder.

JIM

Is that where your mouth is, below your neck and at the start of your arm? What sort of fool do you take me for! How about telling me the truth from the two-lipped orifice on your face!

JOE

That's what I've been doing and I think at the end of the day, when you reflect on what I've been saying, you'll realize that.

JIM

It's now five pm. The sun goes down at seven. I'll see how I feel when the day is over.

JOE

That's fine with me. And I mean that in all sincerity.

JIM

I can't stand this! Shoot me now!

JOE

Is that an honest to God, bona fide, beyond a shadow of a doubt request?

(Jim takes out a gun. The stage goes dark. A shot is heard.)

The Field Guide to People of
the USA

The Field Guide to People of the USA is a user-friendly, fully illustrated manual for identifying varieties of Homo Americanus. Developed by anthropologists, sociologists, and linguists with an interest in featherless bipeds, it is the perfect guidebook to take on walks through America's cities, suburbs, and rural expanses. The following are some entries from the guide. I hope you will find them interesting and informative.

Bigmouth Yenta (Know-It-Allus You-Bet-I-Dous)

Bigmouth yentas think they know all about everything. As a consequence, talking to them is impossible since they can't imagine anyone else would be able to add anything to a conversation. If you are forced into a discussion with a bigmouth yenta just shut up and listen. Eventually they will talk themselves out. *Distinguishing characteristics*: Deeply held beliefs that they know what they are talking about, despite little empirical evidence this is so. *Song*: Inane and endless prattling. *Callnote*: Blah, blah, blah, blah. blah, blah, blah, blah.

Red-Necked Red Neck (Good Old Boyo Americanae)

The red-necked red neck migrates to bars in the winter and NASCAR races and pubs the rest of the year. Dislikes gays, immigrants, and anything French. Rarely strays beyond what they know. *Distinguishing characteristics*: A gun, tattoos, and a conviction that women should be seen and not heard. *Song:* Refrains about fixing trucks, hell-raising, and broken love affairs. *Callnote:* "That dog won't hunt" and "Please don't leave me, darling."

Loose-Lipped Rumormonger (Bogus Storyitis)

Favoring great big whoppers over little white lies, the loose-lipped rumormonger tends to disparage whomever they can. When confronted with their verbal sniping they deny it. Frequently blames others for feeding them false information. *Distinguishing characteristics:* Feelings of great glee in destroying people's reputations and shock when accused of the deed. *Song:* Rapid chattering filled with invective and innuendo. *Callnote:* "Did you hear about . . ."

Nutty American Uncle (Shmucko Idiopathologicum)

Most people have one of these loons amongst their kinfolk. Can often be spotted making inappropriate comments and dancing wildly at weddings and family reunions. Specializes in embarrassing everyone around them. *Distinguishing characteristics:* Engaging in awkward conversations and acting like a total fool. *Song:* Off color jokes and insults. *Callnote:* "Your father never liked me."

Insufferable Woke Millennial (Righteous Paininthe-assus)

This holier-than-thou censor of sin and inequity focuses on pointing out how things have never been worse in American culture. When contradicted with examples of how things were worse in the past, they typically go on Twitter and cancel the person providing those examples. Not fun to be with at parties. *Distinguishing characteristics:* A smug expression and an inability to see people as individuals rather than parts of groups. *Song*: Harangues about the need to be aware of every injustice that has occurred since the dawn of time. *Callnote*: 'Stay woke, no joke."

Dipso Undergraduate (Alcoholus Inebriatu)

This tanked-up student goes to bars at night and sleeps through classes during the day. At spring break they migrate to Fort Lauderdale for round the clock partying. Commonly accompanied by a designated driver and a six-pack. *Distinguishing characteristics*: Unintelligible speech and constant trips to the toilet. *Song*: Hysterical crying and the sharing of inappropriate personal confidences. *Callnote*: "Where the fuck's my beer!"

Hello? Is Anybody There?

Thank you for calling the Department of Motor Vehicles. For English, press one; para español, marque número dos; pour la français, presse trois; für deutsch, drücken sie vier; orfay igpay atinlay, esspray ivefay; для русского, нажмите шесть. Please listen carefully as our menu options have recently changed. If you know your party's extension you may dial it at anytime during this sentence. If you wish to speak to the operator dial "O" but please keep in mind that wishes are only granted in fairytales.

If you would like to participate in a brief survey after this call to help us improve our services press one, if you would rather not participate press two, if you think phone surveys are a total waste of time press three, if you simply feel a need to press something press four.

Is this call related to a matter you are truly worried about? If it is press one and say what is troubling you. If it is not press two, hang up, and have a nice day.

You have pressed one but I can't make out what you said. Please repeat what you said 500,000 times into the phone. Do not rush—speak slowly and carefully. When you have finished speaking press the star key.

I am still having trouble understanding you. Please find someone else to deliver your message or take speech lessons and call back later. I heard you say "no." If that's right press one, if that's not right press two, if you need some more time to think about the question press three. You pressed one so let's do this another way. Rather than mumbling so softly that only a dog would be able to hear you, please scream what you want to say as loudly as you can into the phone. Make sure you are really yelling and not just raising your voice a little.

I believe you said, "the sky is green, the moon is blue, the earth is yellow, the stars chartreuse." If that is what you said press one, if it is not press two. You pressed two, which means you didn't say what I thought you said. No problem, let's try something else.

Please go to your computer and type in the following web address: www.dmvsupport. When the page comes up access the menu bar and click on "Alternative ways to get through to the DMV." While waiting for something to appear on your screen you may want to watch the last season of *Game of Thrones,* read *War and Peace* or a book of similar length, or take a week's vacation in Bermuda.

If you have the patience of Job and the luck of the Irish, you should now be on a page with the heading "I've Got a Question." Below that heading, type in your query and then complete the next 500 pages, which contain interrogatories on every aspect of your life from the date of your conception. Take time composing your answers, as they will be checked for accuracy by a government database that knows you better than you know yourself. When you finish doing this you should be old enough to collect social security. If you are already on social security, congratulations! Future generations may not be as lucky.

The current wait time to speak to a representative is two weeks, six days, seventeen hours, fifteen minutes, and twenty-three seconds. If you would prefer not to wait and instead have someone call you back press one. If you would rather stay in the queue press two. If you would you like a referral to a mental health provider who can offer you coping strategies for dealing with big bureaucracies that could care less about the people they are supposed to serve press three. Thank you for contacting us and have a great day.

Reviewing Paperclips

Your online review will help us to inform other shoppers just like you.

Start by rating it:

5 stars—These are the best paperclips in the world

4 stars—I really like these paperclips

3 stars—They're okay

2 stars—Do they come in different colors?

1 star—I want paperclips made in America

To help us better serve our customers please circle the letter that best corresponds to how you feel about the topic being raised.

1. The reason I bought these paperclips was to:
   a. clip loose papers together
   b. make a key ring
   c. clean my ears
   d. shoot paperclips from rubber bands

2. I purchase paperclips:
   a. when I run out of them
   b. when I can't steal them at work

c. when the moon is in the seventh house and Jupiter aligns with Mars

d. who in their right mind would remember when they last bought paperclips

3. When I do not have a paperclip around to fasten papers I use:
   a. my daughter's nail polish
   b. my son's lacrosse stick
   c. Krazy Glue
   d. The first ten amendments to the US Constitution

4. If you were stranded on a desert island with just a box of paperclips do you think you would:
   a. construct a paperclip boat
   b. build a paperclip sculpture
   c. choreograph a paperclip dance routine
   d. open a clip joint to sucker in the local wildlife

5. The paperclip was invented by:
   a. a college student trying to stay awake in class
   b. a burglar trying to pick a lock
   c. an extraterrestrial with nothing better to do

d. a Twisted Sister

6. I think online surveys are:
   a. a good way for companies to obtain feedback on their products
   b. a fun way for employees to kill time in the office when things are slow
   c. evidence that human beings are moving down the evolutionary ladder
   d. a total waste of time

7. If paperclips ruled the world:
   a. Staples and Office Max would be the powers behind the throne
   b. people would become more sensitive to the feelings of inanimate objects
   c. wars would be fought by Scotch Tape armies using staple guns and box cutters
   d. there would be peace on earth, goodwill to glue

8. If you were to give names to the paperclips on your desk right now, would you:
   a. give them boys' names
   b. give them girls' names

c. ask them what names they would like to be called

d. ask your friends to get you psychiatric help

9. What did the paperclip say to the magnet:

   a. "I think you are very attractive"

   b. "I loved 'Iron Man,' what did you think of the movie?"

   c. "Do you find me repellent?"

   d. Paperclips can't talk, so probably nothing

Thank you for participating in this online survey. We see you also bought legal pads and rubber bands from us and we'd like to know how that worked out. To provide feedback on those purchases please go to www.howarewedoing.com. If we receive your responses within the next two days you will be put on a special list to receive additional surveys on commonplace consumer items for the rest of your life. FYI: You will not be charged for this service.

The Road I Should Not Have Taken

Two highways diverged by a yellow wood,
And sorry I could not travel both
And be one traveler, long I stood
Dithering in my car then thought I could
Ask Siri which one to goeth.

But I took the other, as just as fair,
Not a smart move according to Waze,
Because a police car was waiting there,
Ready to catch speeders who didn't care
How fast they were going to get to a place.

And both that morning equally lay
In asphalt the color of onyx black.
Oh, I really made such a dumb misplay!
I should have driven the other way,
And avoided a ticket and panic attack.

I shall be telling this with a sigh
Somewhere ages and ages hence:
Two highways diverged by a wood, and I—
I stupidly took the one I shouldn't have tried
And that made a monetary difference.

What the F*ck

Fuck this

Fuck that

Fuck no

Fuck yeah

Fuck you

Fuck me

Fuck him

Fuck her

Fucked up

Fuck off

He's fucked

She's fucked

Holy fuck

Mind fuck

Stupid fuck

Silly fuck

Dumb fuck

Clusterfuck

Bumfuck

Fuckhead

Fuckface

Fuckass

Fuckbag

Fuckwad

Fuckhole

Fuckfest

Fuckshow

Fuckjob

Fuckload

Who the fuck

Give a fuck

Fucking stupid

Fucking dumb

Fucking smart

Fucking done

Fucking A

Fucking great

Fucking shit

Motherfucker

Fuck it

Ode to Dorothy Parker

Peanuts can kill you;
Wheat can make you sick;
Shellfish can ill you;
And steak sits like a brick.
Lettuce carries parasites;
Onions make you cry;
Coffee keeps you up at night;
You might as well die.

Photograph By Katherine Liepe-Levinson

PART 3: SELF-HELP

All I Really Need to Know
I Learned in Kindergarten

"All I really need to know I learned in kindergarten." So wrote Robert Fulghum in his best-selling book of the same title. Among the things he learned there were share everything, play fair, clean up your own mess, say you're sorry when you hurt somebody, and don't take things that aren't yours. Well, I learned very different things in kindergarten.

Mrs. Ebeniza Scrooge, my kindergarten teacher, had a teaching philosophy that revolved around the principles of the free market system. She would walk around the classroom and tell us things like: "Purchase gilt-edge securities and hold them." "Buy low, sell high." "Price your goods to move." We had no idea what she was talking about, but those maxims made me tons of money when I became an adult.

Mrs. Scrooge gave us core principles on how to succeed in life and many of them are contrary to the ones Fulghum learned in school. I've found these principles, which I have listed below, quite useful in daily living and if you follow them I have no doubt you will too.

Share as Little as Possible
Whether it's material things or feelings, the less you share with others the more you will have for your own enjoyment. Therefore, unless you are a communist or a masochist, hoard what you can and dole out only what you are forced to give up. Mrs. Scrooge was fond of saying,

"He who dies with the most toys wins." To achieve that objective, keep your playthings to yourself!

Don't Play Fair

It's a truism that nice guys finish last. And the reason they do is because they play fair. Mrs. Scrooge contended that the ends justify the means and if unfairness gets you to your ends, so be it.

Some people find the idea that the ends justify the means a repugnant one. Not Mark Zuckerberg. He believes in making money at all costs and if democracy dies because Facebook will not change the algorithms on its news feed so be it. *E pluribus, screwem*!

Get Others to Clean Up Your Messes

Cleaning up messes is nasty work that should be left to professionals. If you've made a mess of your marriage, speak to an attorney. If you've made a mess of your life, consult a therapist. If you've made a mess in the kitchen, hire a cleaning lady.

Some people believe God helps those who help themselves. Mrs. Scrooge taught us that God also helps those who can get others to help them. If it's good enough for The Almighty it should be good enough for you.

Never apologize when you hurt someone: Apologizing when you hurt someone only adds fuel to the fire. To wit:

Joe: "I'm sorry I hurt your feelings, Mary. I didn't mean to do that."

Mary: "I don't believe you. I think you enjoy insulting me. You get a charge out of it."

Joe: "That's not true. I would never intentionally offend you. I love you."

Mary: "You love me? Then why did you say what you did? Love means never having to say you're sorry."

Joe: "Nevertheless, I am sorry."

Mary: "I'm sorry too. I'm sorry that I met you. Have a nice life, you rotten no-good loser!"

Mrs. Scrooge told us to never apologize, never explain. She said if you injured someone, treat the matter with benign neglect. And if someone injured you, sue the bastard. I've assiduously followed that advice and I can say that as a practicing negligence attorney it has earned me quite a good living. If you ever have a need to litigate, please don't hesitate to call me.

Take what You Can from Others

Mrs. Scrooge taught us that life is like a pie with only so many slices, and each time someone eats a piece there are fewer servings left for everybody else. Consequently, she told us to make sure we got our piece of the pie and while we were at it, to see if we could grab a wedge or two from the folks sitting by us. As Mrs. Scrooge wisely put it, "Those other people shouldn't be eating pie. With all the calories and sugar pie contains, it's not good for them."

I'll always be grateful to Mrs. Scrooge for all that she taught me, and I think if everyone practiced the principles I learned in kindergarten, the world would be a much better place. Flush, wash your hands before you eat, and run roughshod over people wherever and whenever you can. That's sound advice for children and believers in unfettered capitalism.

How Do I Love Me

How do I love me? Let me count the ways.
I love me when I rise at break of day
and I'm staggering around in a haze
searching for car keys that have sadly gone astray.

I love me when I say a careless thing
that I regret cannot be taken back.
I love me when I drop a turkey wing
that falls on the rug and makes a big splat.

I love me freely when I burn the toast.
I love me purely when I stub my toe.
I love me staunchly when I am reproached.
I love me swiftly when I drive too slow.

And if it's my fate to be error prone
I'll love me better till the cows come home.

Consistency Is a Virtue

John Maynard Keynes famously said, "When the facts change, I change my mind. What do you do sir?" I do nothing. Like George W. Bush in Iraq, Lyndon Johnson in Vietnam, and my grandfather in Brooklyn, who smoked two packs of cigarettes a day because doctors in the 1950s said smoking was good for you, I don't flip flop when conditions change. I stay the course because I'd rather be wrong than look stupid.

Throughout human history, many individuals have displayed steadfast determination in the face of overwhelming proof that their positions were nuts. These people had the courage and character to carry on when their take on things was ludicrous. The following vignettes are about four such people who, in their resolve to follow wrongheaded courses of action, show the intrinsic value of staying the course.

Dr. Stewart McStubborn

In the middle of the nineteenth century, Joseph Lister introduced a new way to clean and dress patients' wounds using a solution of carbolic acid. This procedure greatly reduced the number of patients who died from post-operative sepsis infection and was adopted by most surgeons. But not by Dr. Stewart McStubborn, the chief of surgery at the You Bet Your Life Clinic in Glasgow, Scotland. He stubbornly kept doing what he had always done—letting wounds fester. As a result, he was able to maintain that great medical tradition encapsulated in the phrase "the operation was successful, but the patient died." And, because he collected his fees upfront, he was also able to maintain a prosperous medical practice.

Commodore Horatio Bullhead

In the America's Yacht Club race of 1898, Commodore Horatio Bullhead tied the sails down on his vessel so they wouldn't move in any direction. He thought by doing this, his boat would stay the course and he'd win the race.

Before the competition, the other skippers warned Bullhead that if he bound his sails his boat would capsize and sink in the event of very strong winds. Bullhead laughed in their sunburnt faces, saying, "You guys can tack your sails and zigzag all over the ocean. My sails are set and I'm heading straight for the finish line."

There were powerful winds on the day of the race and, true to the prediction of the other captains, Bullhead's yacht rolled over and went to the bottom. Luckily for Bullhead he was rescued by another boat. When he was safely aboard that craft, its commander asked how he felt. Bullhead replied, "I feel fine because there's more to life than winning a race. There's staying the course for what you believe in." The other captain said, "Those words would make a great foundation for a political campaign speech. You should run for office somewhere."

Bullhead ran for Congress in the state where he lived and won a resounding victory. He served in the House of Representatives for twenty years, earning a boatload of money from lobbyists and corporate bigwigs whose interests he advanced. Clearly good things can happen if you stay the course.

Rick Reticent

Rick Reticent was a huge star in the days of silent movies, appearing in more than eighty films including the silent classic *I'll Scream Tomorrow*. When the talkies came along Rick didn't flip-flop and abandon the genre in which he had become famous. He told the press, "I'm a silent movie actor. I will not speak in front of the camera. I owe that to my fans."

Keeping mute was not a great career move for Reticent, and before you could say "1n 1927, *The Jazz Singer* helped make talkies a global phenomenon," he was forced to leave the film industry. However, he was a big enough star that he landed a job as a mannequin at Macy's. During World War II, Reticent often appeared at War Bonds rallies, where he silently implored the audience to buy bonds.

General Maxime von Kookoo

In 1943, German tanks attacked Belgian general Maxime von Kookoo and 500 horse cavalry under his command. The battle has since become known as "Kookoo's Last Stand," an apt name for the encounter, as von Kookoo and his men were completely wiped out.

Von Kookoo's military role model was Genghis Khan, a thirteenth-century emperor who swept across Asia with a mounted Mongol army to conquer two-thirds of the known world. Though warfare had changed quite a bit in 700 years, von Kookoo refused to compromise his faith in the efficacy of the horse-borne cavalry charge. The last words this noble soldier uttered were, "If wishes were horses, then tanks would be too."

Five Hot Stock Picks for the Coming Year

Investing in stocks can be a great way of earning life-changing wealth. The trick is to pick stocks that go up rather than move in the opposite direction. That's easier said than done; but not for professional stock pickers, who because of their great financial acumen and knowledge of the stock market invariably know the best stocks to buy. The following are five such stocks. Buy them now or live with the thought that you could have made a ton of dough if you had the guts to follow the advice of people who know what they're doing.

Meshuganah Exploration and Mining

Everyone wants to look young and live as long as possible and that makes this company an excellent investment, as it is seeking the Fountain of Youth, a legendary spring that reputedly restores the youth of anyone who drinks its waters. Meshuganah miners are currently drilling for the fountain in Florida, which history points to as the most likely location, and in the backyard of the actor George Hamilton. If these places do not pan out, another area being considered for exploration is the attic of Dorian Gray. With Meshuganah there is more than just light at the end of the tunnel. There are massive loads of money.

BS Power and Lighting Company

BS Power and Lighting is heavily involved in researching alternative energy sources. The company is currently working on a device that converts the hot air generated from commercial advertising and political campaigns into usable power. If they are successful in this venture the world will be guaranteed a perpetual source of sustainable energy, and the bull**** from the ads and political speeches we all have to endure will have some real value. They say money talks and BS walks, but if this business succeeds in discovering a substitute for oil it's going to fly like the wind. Set your sails high, let go of your lines, and grab this stock now!

JetRed

To make money in the airline biz you need to keep your expenses down and cram lots of people into your planes. *JetRed* excels in both these areas.

To contain costs the company does not employ pilots or flight attendants. Instead, its planes are programmed to fly on instruments and passengers are given safety instructions and a bag of peanuts when they board at the gate.

To maximize customer load, JetRed offers discount passenger seating in the cockpit and in lavatories—those who opt for such seats must know either how to make small talk over a loudspeaker system or how to convince people not to go to the bathroom. There is also a reduced-price straphanger option for folks willing to stand in the aisles and there are deeply discounted seats in the cargo compartment.

Airline industry analysts are predicting that JetRed should make lots of money this year if the weather is good and there is not much turbulence in the atmosphere, conditions the *Farmer's Almanac* says will occur. The skies ahead look bright and sunny for JetRed. Its stock is poised for a rapid ascent.

The Mime Group

There has been noise on the street that this silent bunch of black-suited buskers is about to move to the next financial level. It's easy to see why. For one thing, the group's revenue comes in the form of loose change and dollar bills, so the business has easy access to cash. In addition, many of the firm's principals have other jobs, which means the moolah they make from miming is pure profit that can go toward shareholder dividends. Mime's management is keeping mum about the group's prospects for the coming year, but those in the know say this company is definitely worth a shout-out.

Bon Mots "R" Us

This French-owned concern devises clever words and expressions to describe people, places, and things. In response to a request for a phrase to portray a leader who invades another country on false pretenses, *Bon Mots "R" Us* came up with the word "Putinesca." During the Trump era, when a request was made for a locution to capture the revulsion that much of the world felt for America's president, they combined English and Yiddish to produce the term "Whatadumbschmuck." The company is currently working on an expression to describe a country that has reneged on its promise to buy French submarines.

Please note that this is a French corporation and there is more risk involved in foreign investing. However, France has been around for a long time and the French people, when they're not taking long vacations at the beach or lounging in cafes, tend to be pretty good workers. Stock market professionals who are into linguistic niceties consider Bon Mots a "supercalifragilisticexpialidocious" buy.

Retirement Ideas for the Young

Young people are saving less than their parents did at the same age. This could be a problem when they are ready to retire, as they may not have enough money to enjoy their golden years. The following four ideas can help to avert such a catastrophe.

Make Sure Your Parents Like You

Some parents leave their money to their children for no other reason than the love and obligation they feel that comes with the parent-child relationship. But other parents feel no such duty. They may bequeath their money to a favorite relative, their alma mater, or the Society for the Perpetuation of Portuguese Petunias.

To make sure your parents' inheritance doesn't go to a bunch of interlopers, you need to make sure your parents like you. This means you must listen sympathetically to your father's rants against the federal government and your mother's complaints about your father never helping around the house. You must send a card to your parents on their anniversary and let them rag on your significant other or spouse if you have one. If you have left the nest and return home because you were fired from your job or your partner has called it quits, offer to rinse the dishes and clear the table after dinner. With any sort of luck, if you've taken my advice, you will be clearing a lot more than crumbs from a counter down the road.

Reduce Your Spending

If you live by the motto "a penny saved is a penny earned" you will be able to accumulate a nice piece of change by the time you are ready to retire. But with so many great things to buy in the world it can be hard to save one's pennies. That's okay, because doing difficult things develops character.

You can start to save by not buying clothing. Instead, hang around Salvation Army drop-off bins and tell people who are donating clothes there that they should donate them to you because charity begins at home and home is where you're going.

Forget about purchasing an expensive set of wheels. Join the army and they'll let you drive pricey vehicles for nothing. While it's true soldiers' salaries aren't very high, the death benefit has recently been raised, which brings up a big plus for military service. If you are killed in action you won't have to worry about retirement.

Finally, to save on food expenses, cut down on the number of meals you consume. Lots of people don't eat breakfast; plenty of folks skip lunch; and missing dinner never killed anybody. A snack at noon and one in the evening is sufficient to survive on till you reach the age for social security, at which point you can celebrate with a big banquet.

Work More

There are 168 hours in a seven-day week and I'm sure you're not working all of them. Well, get cracking! Figure out the number of hours you need to eat, sleep, and take care of other bodily functions and subtract that number from 168. Then find yourself employment for the rest of the time.

There's a twofold advantage to working round the clock—you will make more money if you work more hours and that additional sum can be saved, and if you are constantly working you won't have time to buy anything.

There's one small negative to working more hours. You may become exhausted and die on the job. But this can also be a positive because, as was mentioned earlier, kicking the bucket at work means you won't have to worry about providing for your golden years.

Become a Member of Congress

Government pensions are here to stay and one of the best ways to collect one is to become a member of Congress, a job that offers not just a pension but other great benefits like being able to go on TV and telling everyone how the world should be run, receiving kickbacks from businesses currying your vote, going on travel junkets, and getting free postage. Moreover, unlike other federal employees, people in Congress can increase their pensions by voting themselves pay raises. But you better start running for office soon because if these perks become more widely known there may be increased competition for the job.

Cognitive Biases to Clear Thinking

A cognitive bias refers to systematic errors in one's thinking. Such biases can skew perceptions and impair rational thought. The biases discussed below do particular damage in those areas.

Thinking for Yourself

This bias goes against the common sense notion best expressed in the cliché "Fifty million Frenchmen can't be wrong and a hundred million Frenchmen are twice as likely to be right." Those who exhibit this bias voice dissenting opinions during discussions and think it's okay to stand out from the group. This makes them impossible to talk to and a pain in the ass in getting things done. These folks refuse to *go along to get along*, preferring instead to *call 'em as they sees 'em*, which is a fine philosophy for a baseball umpire but a disaster if you're working in a bureaucracy or with any set of people.

Anyone with half a brain knows that the wisdom of the crowd far surpasses the understanding found in any individual person. Shakespeare had it right when he said, "To thine own self be true but when dealing with others, be true to the herd."

The Fallacy that Less is More

The idea that less is more is less than smart and more than dumb. Why is that you ask? It's because we live in the

United States of America, a capitalist, consumer-driven society where the right approach to living is *more is more*.

It is ill mannered and unpatriotic to not want more than your neighbors, your relatives, your co-workers, and everyone else in the world. What do you think would happen if we all bought fewer goods and didn't care about making lots of money? The answer is the American economy would go into the toilet and no one would be able to afford a plumber to fix the damn thing. The only time the notion "less is more" makes any sense is when a person wants to do less walking and more driving because motoring to places leads to gas purchases, parking fees, and the increased buying of vehicles.

The Misconception that There are Alternatives

Making decisions in everyday life is a two-horse race that only gets confusing if you add more ponies. For example, let's say you're on a date and the subject comes up about where to go after dinner. The choices should be obvious: you can go to either their place or yours. Consider other options and you may never wind up in bed.

Or let's say you're having a discussion with someone, and it turns into an argument. Should you spend time trying to find common ground you both can agree on? Of course not! There are two sides to every argument and if you're an able persuader your side should prevail. You're either with me or against me, it's true or it's not, you're a success or a failure, they love you or they don't. Make a choice, take a stand, and forget about anything else.

125

The Misbelief that if You Have Nothing to Say, Say Nothing

Verbal expression is the mirror of the mind and if you have nothing to say in a situation people will see in that mirror the image of an idiot. Moreover, it is a given in American culture that one should have views and opinions on everything, and that includes stuff one is clueless about. Saying, "I don't know" when asked a question is the same thing as saying, "You are speaking to a fool."

The less you know about a matter the more you should talk about it, as it really does not matter what you say about a matter but that you are mattering to venture a thought. If you pontificate well and often enough about things you know nothing about you may be called on to do guest appearances on radio and TV talk shows. From there, who knows where your ignorance will take you.

How to Deal with Difficult People

Some people are just difficult to get along with. No matter what you do to be nice to them they resist your pleas, which may lead you to become sullen or sulk, act defensively or attack. But you don't have to behave self-protectively with difficult people. Use the guaranteed, foolproof strategies listed below and you will stay calm, get what you want, and keep your dignity.

Dealing with Hostile-Aggressive People

The main rule in dealing with hostile-aggressive individuals is "don't back down." If you do they will walk all over you and I don't mean in a sweet shiatsu sort of way. They will stomp on your ego and trample your self-esteem if you give them half a chance. Therefore don't give them a half a chance. Give them *no* chance.

The following scenario, between Ms. Jones (a customer-service representative) and Mr. Smith (a buyer), offers instruction on how to deal with a hostile-aggressive person.

Ms. Jones: I'm sorry, Mr. Smith, but Mr. Peters isn't in today. He left two hours ago for LA.

Mr. Smith: What do you mean he isn't in? I just flew half way across the country to see him. We had a meeting scheduled to talk about a new line of goods I want to buy from your company.

Jones: I've checked with Mr. Peters' calendar and it shows you're booked to see him next week. I'm sure . . .

Smith: I don't want to hear lies and excuses. The customer is always right. You're a total moron and your com-

127

pany sucks. What are you going to do make this right, you stupid, ignorant, jackass!

Jones: I'll be happy to tell you what I'm going to do. I am going to make a call to *Ice Pick Willie's Pizza-and-contract-for-hire Brasserie* and tell them to deliver 400 pizzas to your house if you don't fly back here within a week after you get home. Then I'm making a note on my calendar to call your wife to tell her we are having an affair if you don't get your butt back here in the next seven days. For the nonce, I am going to lunch. When I return from eating, I will take you to the airport so you can return whence you came and reserve plane tickets to visit us next week. Is there anything else I can do for you?

Smith: Yes. Please don't call Ice Pick Willie's or my wife.

Jones: I won't do those things if you're back here within the time parameters I have laid out. Have a nice day.

Dealing with Complainers

Complainers are whining, self-righteous malcontents who manage to find fault with everything. The disguised message in their complaints is that you should do something about their gripes. Actually, you would like to do something, but not about their gripes. You would like to move to China so you wouldn't have to listen to their constant moaning. But there are moaners in China too, so I suggest studying the example that follows and use the tactic of "out complaining the complainer" as a way to handle the problem.

Mr. Brown: It's always cold in this office. Why don't they give us heat when we come to work?

Ms. Miller: There's always so much traffic when I commute in the morning. Why can't there be less traffic on the road?

Brown: What does your commute have to do with the lack of heat in the office?

Miller: I hate it when people ask stupid questions. Don't you?

Brown: What are you talking about? You're not making sense to me.

Miller: Why is gas so expensive? Why do politicians lie all the time? Why does it cost so much to get into the Museum of Modern Art? Why doesn't our company give us raises?

Brown: You're making me uncomfortable with all your complaining. How about we both quit talking for a while?

Miller: Okay. Let's speak again at lunch. Then again, maybe we can't. I heard the employees' cafeteria is closed today for renovations. Why don't they do that work on weekends? Why doesn't management allow us to have flextime schedules? Why did our union negotiate such a lousy contract? . . .

Dealing with Negativists

Negativists are people who answer any proposal with an explanation like "It won't work" or "It's no use trying" or "Forget it, they'll never let us do it." These doomsayers drag everybody down with their hopelessness and despair.

One way to deal with negativists is to try to make them feel guilty for asserting their non-constructive views. To wit:

Facilitator. We've been reviewing this problem for months. I think it's time we start to solve it.

Negativist. You'd better think again. The higher-ups around here don't want us to solve the problem. They want us to spin our wheels. Besides, this problem is too complex to figure out. We're wasting our time even discussing it.

Facilitator. Thanks for the feedback. Your pessimism is duly noted. Now let's get to work on a solution to the problem.

Negativist. How can we come up with a solution to a problem that can't be solved? Let's give it a rest and go to lunch.

Facilitator. Maybe eating is all we should ever do. Maybe we should never bother to go forward with anything in life. What's the sense of doing things when in the end we're all doomed to go into the abyss? I wonder why any of us shows up for work at all. Shakespeare was right—life is but a walking shadow, a poor player who struts and frets his hour upon the stage and then is heard no more. I'm going to kill myself. Why go on living!

Negativist. Hey, not so fast. Life isn't that bad. There are lots of things to live for.

Facilitator. I can see only one. Trying to solve the problem we've been talking about. If you can't help me to do that, I see no way out other than doing myself in. We either try to come up with a solution to the problem or I jump out the window right now. What's it to be? My fate is in your hands.

Negativist. All right, for God's sake. I'll help you solve the damn problem. Just don't do anything rash.

Facilitator. Thanks. You saved my life. Lunch is on me today.

Defeat Low Self-Esteem

Self-esteem is the opinion you have of yourself. If that opinion is low, you will have problems getting motivated and being successful. Fortunately, a poor sense of self-esteem can be reversed. In fact, it can't survive if you follow these suggestions:

Don't Indulge in Self-Criticism

Let's say you've invaded a country in the Middle East and things have gone badly—the residents there are fighting with each other, the government you installed is corrupt, your reason for the invasion was proven spurious, and your poll numbers are tanking back home. Don't admit to that person in the mirror that you've botched the situation by not planning more carefully! Don't wage war against yourself! Silence your inner critic and hope in a hundred years it will all have been forgotten.

Don't Try to be Like Someone Else

Trying to be like someone else can lead to a lack of self-worth and self-confidence. Remember, you are unique. You can strive to be better, yes, but don't criticize yourself for not being as successful, as attractive, as smart, or as popular as some other person. You are just fine being who you are—an unsuccessful, unattractive, dumb, loathsome loser who wants to kill themself. But here's a good thing: with all those negative characteristics there's no place to go but up.

You Can Choose to Please Yourself Before Others

Imagine you are a member of Congress and a defense industry lobbyist offers you a bag of cash to support building submarines that can dance, whistle, and sing songs. You could really use the dough, because it's tough to support a wife, two mistresses, and a drug habit on a government salary. But you have some qualms about backing a product that seems ridiculous on its face. Well, it's nice that you care about wasteful spending, but aren't *your* needs important? Of course they are. Take the money and run.

Failure is Not a Permanent Condition

Failure simply means you are not successful YET. Everybody fails on their way up. Donald Trump was an incompetent and inept businessman for many years. But he saw failure as a means to learning. With God's help, and with the assistance of a reality TV show, FOX news, and the Russians, Trump engineered a dramatic change of direction and became President of the United States. Problems can make you stronger if you strive to overcome them.

As Dumb As You Are, There Are Others Who Are Dumber

There are more than seven billion people living on earth, so even if you're a world-class dimwit it's more than likely there are a few other people on the globe dumber than you. Hey, are you as dumb as the captain of the Titanic, who didn't slow his ship when he was warned of icebergs in its path? Are you as dumb as George Armstrong Custer, who against the advice of his scouts split up his small force and was massacred with a few hundred other US cavalrymen at the Little Bighorn? Are you as dumb as Paris Hilton, who said, "What's WalMart; do they sell, like, wall stuff?" Probably not, so relax and don't be so hard on yourself. That's dumb.

Five Effective Communication Strategies

We all want to communicate effectively. But to do that takes more than just desire. It takes effective strategies, such as the five that will now be discussed.

Never Put It in Writing

Joe sends Tom, Dick, and Harry an email containing the words "Have a nice day," meaning for them to have a pleasant twenty-four hours. But that's not how they interpret the message. Tom thinks, "Have a nice day is such a meaningless expression. I bet Joe says that to all the people he corresponds with." Dick's take is, "How come Joe didn't tell me to have a *great* day? Why did he wish me just a nice one?" And Harry supposes, "Joe's a jerk. He knows I'm dealing with lots of difficult problems. How can I have a nice day with all the stuff I have to handle?"

The fact is, anything you write to someone will be misconstrued. And, as we have just seen, that includes phrases as innocuous as "Have a nice day." Therefore, if an urge comes upon you to write something to somebody wait till that desire disappears. Better yet, type whatever it is you want to say into your computer, save it, and forget about it. Even better, delete it! If you save it someone might discover and read it, and you know what that means.

Say As Little As Possible

As with writing, whatever you tell someone will be misjudged. However, unlike writing, you will *immediately* be given a hard time for saying it. Therefore, keep your mouth shut and simply listen during conversations. To not fall asleep when the other person is talking, nod your head up and down every fifteen seconds or so. That should give you plenty of time to daydream and focus on your own thoughts. If you get bored with all the head bobbing tell the other individual, "I see what you're getting at." Gives the same results.

Don't Move

As with writing and speaking, others will misread whatever you communicate nonverbally. If you cross your arms because that feels comfortable, people will think you're angry. If you cross your legs because that also feels good, people will think you're withholding. If you smile because you want to be friendly, people will think you're an idiot.

One way to minimize the chance that others will misinterpret your nonverbal cues is to die. Dead people, because of their lack of movement, usually do not confuse the living with their gestures. If that communication strategy does not appeal to you, try to shift around as little as possible when talking with others. If you're into yoga, assume the corpse position in discussions. Alternatively, claim you suffer from narcolepsy and take a nap.

Live on a Deserted Island

Living on a deserted island is an excellent way to reduce the possibilities for human misunderstanding, as there won't be anybody around to get wrong ideas about what you want to convey. Write, talk, behave however you like; if you're by yourself, no one can take offense. However, be careful not to yell at or make abrupt gestures to creatures on the island who are bigger or who have sharper teeth than you because misconceptions on their part may prove fatal. Try to engage such animals in card games and make sure that you lose.

Speak Softly and Carry a Big Stick

President Theodore Roosevelt successfully used this communication strategy at the beginning of the twentieth century. Employing it, he was able to convince the Colombian government to let America build the Panama Canal, persuade rebels in the Philippines to give up their insurgency, and induce Mrs. Roosevelt to have his breakfast ready when he got up in the morning. If you adopt this strategy you might want to consider carrying a book of postmodern poetry rather than a big stick. A book is less obtrusive and nothing beats threatening to read postmodern verse to get people to pay attention to you.

You Gotta Love Winning

I like to start off each day with a victory. So this morning, before I left for the office, I beat my wife to the bathroom and my kids out the door and as a result one of them had to walk the dog. Those triumphs put a spring in my step and some joy in my heart as I strode to the subway. I agree with Vince Lombardi, "Winning isn't everything, it's the only thing."

The train was about to leave when I reached the platform, but I was able to get my hands between the closing doors of one of the cars, which meant the conductor had a choice to make—release the doors and let me in or keep them shut and hope I'd withdraw my meat hooks. That second option was never a possibility. After a ten-minute standoff the conductor threw in the towel and I entered the train with a big smile on my face and two very red and swollen mitts. Benjamin Franklin was right in his observation, "No pain, no gain."

At work, I went over to Bill Johnson's computer and signed him up for subscriptions to twenty-five different magazines to be delivered to his home. Bill had embarrassed me in front of the boss three times in a row and I had to get my revenge. Robert F. Kennedy put it best, "Never get mad, get even."

Back in my office I received a call from one of our customers. He was unhappy with an order that had been sent to him and wanted his money back. I told him we would send him a new batch of goods but we wouldn't refund his dough. We argued back and forth for over an hour but in the end my threat to abduct him and make

137

him watch reruns of the Jerry Springer Show won him over to my position. Dwight D. Eisenhower knew what he was talking about when he said, "No one can defeat us unless we first defeat ourselves."

To celebrate my morning's conquests, I went to Dan's Diner for lunch and ordered the meatloaf special. Sadly, they had run out of meatloaf. When I asked Dan if he would let me have the fish for the same price as the meatloaf special, he said no. It wasn't the money that mattered to me, it was the chance to compete. So I told Dan if he didn't give me a discount on the fish I would put signs up all over the neighborhood dissing his diner, I would hire a lawyer to sue him for false advertising, and I would picket his place on the weekends. Realizing he was up against a force mightier than himself, Dan reluctantly took a couple bucks off the price of the fish, thus confirming Winston Churchill's advice to "Never give in. Never, never, never, never—in nothing great or small."

In the afternoon, I made a chump out of my administrative assistant when he claimed the state capital of Alaska was Anchorage. When I told him he didn't know what he was talking about, and that he should stick to typing and filing, he offered to bet me fifty dollars that Anchorage was Alaska's capital. Since I had been stationed in Juneau, the capital of Alaska, when I was in the service, I took that bet and rubbed it in real good when Google showed he was wrong. What joy it is to crush the opposition! Billy Martin told no lies when he said, "Everything looks nicer when you win. The girls are prettier. The cigars taste better. The trees are greener."

On my way home I was mugged by a couple of punks who pulled out guns and ordered me to give them my wallet. Fat chance I was going to do that. I lunged for the first guy, grabbed his weapon, and shot the poor bastard. But the second mug got off a couple of lucky shots that mortally wounded me and made me miss my dinner. However, the jerk ran off without taking my cash, so technically I defeated him. While this may have been a Pyrrhic victory, as I was going to die in the next few hours, that's a victory too, and that fact is essential because, in the words of football coach George Allen, "When you win you're reborn." That means I'm coming back.

You gotta love winning!

Baby Boomer Love

Question: How can I tell if I'm ready to date after a divorce or separation?

"When the idea of getting to know a new person feels better than drinking all day and crying all night, you're probably ready to start dating." So says Lucy Love, the author of the bestselling book *It's a Meet Market Out There*. "If thoughts of dating start with 'I want' rather than 'I should,' consider this a signal that you're ready to test the waters. But be careful not to get in over your head. Start with your big toe and work your way slowly into the dating pool. If you meet someone with a foot fetish you could get lucky right away."

Question: Should I fudge my age to seem more attractive to prospects?

"Dishonesty is the best policy if you care about having long-term relationships," advises Holly Hokum, webmistress of SexySeniors.com. "If the person you're dating turns out to be a good fit, do you want to risk your relationship with the truth? Young is in, and the younger you tell others you are the more in you will be. Just don't say you're under sixteen. Makes you jailbait."

Question: Where are the best places to meet people I'd click with? I'm so over the bar scene.

Dr. Ruth Eastheimer, noted psychotherapist and author of *Sex and Death: The First Is More Fun,* says, "Go to real-estate open houses, lectures at the local university, the pool in your apartment complex, group orgies, swinger conventions, whatever. The point is to try new things that interest you but also to be open to opportunities in your everyday life. With respect to the people I counsel, group orgies and swinger conventions are part of everyday life."

Question: How do I tell my grown kids I'm starting to date? I'm worried they won't approve of me going out.

Brooklyn-based psychologist Sigmoid Freud says, "Simply tell your children, 'I'm starting to date.' If your kids respond by giving you a hard time, tell them your doctor has said you have six months to live and you want to enjoy yourself in the remaining days you have on Earth. If they continue to harass you, tell them to stick it where the sun don't shine. You're too old for this sort of aggravation."

Question: As a guy, what should I say if my date and I start to get intimate and I have performance issues?

Mack Truck, the author of *Bed 'em, Don't Wed 'em* says, "A sense of humor can take you far in this case—laugh it off and your date probably will too. However, impotence is really nothing to titter over. If watching porn or taking Viagra doesn't work, I'd consider suicide. Who'd want to live with such humiliation!"

Horoscope Predictions for The Goddess that You Are

Capricorn (Dec. 22—Jan. 19)

Next week you will meet the man of your dreams. He'll be working at the deli counter in your local BJ's and wearing a white uniform and white paper hat. He will ask you if you want your bologna sliced thin. Smile demurely and ask him what he would suggest. If he says, "I don't give advice on matters like that, I just cut the meat the way the customer tells me to" he's the wrong guy. It's the fellow next to him who's the man of your dreams.

Best day to go food shopping: Any day you are running low on food. Don't forget to make a list of what you need before you go out and wear something pretty. Your dreamboat will appreciate that.

Taurus (Apr. 20—May 20)

WOW, WOW, and triple WOW!!! Time to quit your job because you are going to win the lottery. You will be able to do whatever you want for the rest of your life. How about lending me five G's. I promise to pay you back with interest.

Best day to spoil yourself: Any day you feel like it.

Cancer (June 21—July 22)

Flirt alert! Your ex from college will bring love into your life, if you're open to it. However that love will come with a hitch, as Chad has become a Mafia hit man and is running from the law. But there's an upside! If the relationship turns sour you'll be able to turn Chad over to the authorities for a big reward.

Best day to join the Witness Protection Program: The day you call the cops on Chad.

Leo (July 23—Aug. 22)

Spotlight, please! You're a knockout from the 24th to the 30th, thanks to powerhouse Pluto and the $150,000 you've invested in plastic surgery. Wear a dazzling outfit and create conversation to match. You've got a one-week window to snag Mr. Right. Don't blow it.

Best day to celebrate: When he gives you that ring.

Virgo (Aug. 23—Sept. 22)

Time to redecorate! Your home is your castle but where are the regal accouterments, my queen? Do you have a throne, red carpet, inner and outer walls, a gate-house, and a moat? No! What are you waiting for? Build your royal palace and the princes will come.

Best day for a royal wedding: Monday-Sunday.

Mister Etiquette: The Dark Side

Dear Mister Etiquette:

I recently received an invitation to go to a cousin's engagement party but I have never met this cousin and will be busy the day of the celebration. Must I send them a gift?

~Perplexed about the right thing to do

Dear Perplexed:

There is no one right thing to do in such a case. Your cousin may genuinely want you to participate in their happy event or he or she may simply be trolling for gifts. I have a somewhat jaundiced view of human nature so I suspect the latter. Therefore, ignore the invitation and with the money you save on buying a present take yourself out to a restaurant and have a nice meal. When the dessert comes, toast to your cousin's good fortune and hope you are not invited to the wedding.

Dear Mister Etiquette:

When I sit down to eat at a fancy affair, I often get confused about what silverware to use and which glasses to drink from. Do you have any advice that can help me survive formal dinners?

~Not wishing to make a faux pas

Dear Faux pas Avoider:

I, too, sometimes get confused about which silverware and glasses to use at fancy affairs, particularly if I have imbibed heavily during the cocktail hour. So I often wait until my fellow diners begin to eat and then simply copy what they do.

If you use a utensil that was supposed to be employed later in the meal and the server removed it before you could stop him or her do not despair. Tell your dining companions that you see smoke at the far end of the room and while they are looking for the fire, swipe the same utensil from the tableware set out in front of the person seated next to you. Remember, at formal functions the rule is you are what you eat, with.

Dear Mister Etiquette:

Is it considered good manners for a man to hold the door open for a woman or has that behavior gone the way of the dodo bird?

~A mystified and puzzled gentleman

Dear Mystified:

The jury is out on that question. However, one way to skirt the issue is to wear casts on both your arms. Then the ladies will have to hold the door open for you. If this solution is not appealing try to avoid being with females who go in and out of places. While doing that will probably leave you with only homeless women as companions, the fact is those gals could probably use some company.

If you find yourself in a situation where you and a woman reach the door at the same time you might want to attempt this maneuver: hold the door open for her and then turn around and scream as loud as you can, "Would anyone else like to come in!" This will likely cause the lady to think you are a lunatic rather than a male chauvinist pig who thinks women don't have the strength to open doors for themselves. If she takes pity on you because she is a nice person and sees lunacy as a disability, you might consider asking her out for a drink. If she accepts your offer, take her to a place with people coming in and out constantly so someone can hold the door open for both of you.

Influencers from the Bible

Today's lesson from the Bible is about the role of influencers in getting people to do one's bidding. The Good Book is filled with examples of such individuals—and animals. Exhibit A: the serpent in the Garden of Eden who through an appeal to wanting to be as smart as God convinced Eve to eat an apple from the tree of knowledge.

Eve #MoreThanJustaRib was the first human influencer. She persuaded the only other person living in the world at the time to take a bite of an apple she had just bitten into. As a result of those bites the pair was forced to quit the gardening business and find other lines of work, which they did, specifically in real estate relocation, men's and women's apparel, and human reproduction. Eve's rise (or fall) from horticulturist to entrepreneur and mother of humanity is a charming and instructive story that can't be told too often.

Delilah #Dscrissorhands was a hottie from Sorek who was paid by the lords of the Philistines to use her influencing skills to uncover the source of her boyfriend's strength. To do this she micro-targeted her partner with messages that played to his male vanity, to wit: "I like my men strong and sensitive. How did you get to be that way?" "You got a great head of hair and I can understand why you wouldn't want to cut it but if you did I'm sure the world wouldn't come crashing down on you." "I tell you all my secrets but you seem a bit withholding. How about telling me the secret of your strength?"

Delilah's persistent efforts to uncover her boyfriend's physical prowess, which she was successful at, paid off handsomely. Her brand awareness rose to such as extent that the writers of the Old Testament included her as a character in the Bible, and while that inclusion was not an especially flattering one no publicity is bad publicity. Being mentioned in a book that has been read by billions of people for thousands of years gave Delilah immortality, which is something most folks would die for.

Noah #aHighandDryGuy was a righteous man who walked with God. He was also a big-time animal influencer with tremendous organizational skills who the Lord turned to when he became upset about how the world had become corrupt and filled with violence. Irritated beyond all that is holy, God told Noah to build an Ark in which he, his sons, and their wives together with male and females of all living creatures would be saved from a flood that God was going to cause on earth.

Noah got right on the case, direct messaging all the animals on the planet through twitter—natural bird calls not the social networking service that people use today. The message he sent asked them to select representatives of their species to come on board the Ark. Because Noah was one of God's faves, and a PETA contributor, they complied with his request. The upshot was the human race was saved and Noah's story, besides being an essential part of the Bible, was made into a movie starring Russell Crowe and Emma Watson—FYI the film can be streamed on Prime.

Moses #LetMyPeopleGo was one of the Bible's most prolific influencers, persuading Pharaoh to let the Jews go from Egypt and convincing the Hebrews to accept the Ten Commandments. To accomplish the former, he enlisted God's help in incentivizing the Egyptians to free the Jews through the selective use of plagues. That plan worked and Moses wound up with thousands of followers who agreed to leave their homes and take a road trip to Mount Sinai where God gave them the Torah, a five-book series packed with divine revelation.

The day after the Torah giving, God told Moses to hike up to the top of Mount Sinai where the Lord would give him two stone tablets on which the Ten Commandments were carved. Moses did so but his followers, too impatient to wait for their leader to come back off the mountain and depressed by skies made dark by Satan (a Biblical influencer who is always up to no good), reneged on their pledge to monotheism and started to worship a golden calf. When Moses finally rejoined his rebellious disciples he became angry and smashed the tablets he was carrying.

God directed Moses to chisel out two new tablets and, after God rewrote them, share their contents with the Jews. Moses obeyed the Lord's injunction and was able to get the Israelites to see that a belief in one God, not committing adultery, and honoring one's parents was trending all across Sinai and fast becoming a meme. Long story short, the children of Israel #TheChosenPeople updated their religious views and marched 40 years across the wilderness to reach the Holy Land. Moses did not go with them because the big boss had canceled him for breaking faith. Moses died within sight of Canaan on Mount Nebo, where his avatar is still trying to get into Israel.

Next week we will cover the upsides and downsides of miracles. Be prepared to take notes and see those notes fly up to the sky and turn into clouds. Bring an umbrella in case some of those clouds start pouring down rain as you are on your way to class. You may also want to bring a list of things you desire in life, which, if time permits, you can ask God for at the end of the lesson.

About the Author

Martin H. Levinson does not teach creative writing at Stanford. In 2022, he was not awarded a MacArthur Genius Grant or a spot on the "20 under 40" *New Yorker* writer's list. He has never written seven *New York Times* bestsellers nor won a Nobel Prize in Literature. He lives with his wife and his hopes for a saner world in the current millennium. He is grateful for the recognition he has not sought or received and plans to continue to work in utter obscurity.